CW00816260

1 MONTH OF
FREE
READING

at

www.ForgottenBooks.com

By purchasing this book you are eligible for one month membership to ForgottenBooks.com, giving you unlimited access to our entire collection of over 1,000,000 titles via our web site and mobile apps.

To claim your free month visit:
www.forgottenbooks.com/free226487

ISBN 978-0-483-42284-1
PIBN 10226487

THE FAITH AND MODERN THOUGHT

SIX LECTURES

BY

WILLIAM TEMPLE

HEADMASTER OF REPTON ; CHAPLAIN TO THE ARCHBISHOP OF CANTERBURY
FORMERLY FELLOW OF QUEEN'S COLLEGE, OXFORD

WITH INTRODUCTION BY M. E. SADLER

MACMILLAN AND CO., LIMITED
ST. MARTIN'S STREET, LONDON

1913

RICHARD CLAY AND SONS, LIMITED,
BRUNSWICK STREET, STAMFORD STREET, S.E.,
AND BUNGAY, SUFFOLK.

CONTENTS

LECTURE I

LECTURE II

AUTHOR'S NOTE

As it was desired that these Lectures should appear as soon as possible, I have only edited the report made at their delivery, and have not changed a form comparatively appropriate, as I hope, for the spoken word into one more suitable for print. Where nothing is original it is idle to specify obligations.

W. T.

INTRODUCTION

THE lectures printed in this volume were delivered, under the auspices of the London Intercollegiate Christian Unions, in St. James's Hall, London, during November and December, 1909, to audiences of men and women students of the University. They are now issued in a form convenient for use by those who desire to study the fundamental problems of the Christian Faith.

Those who heard the course were impressed by the personality of the lecturer, by the simplicity of his words, the candour of his reasoning and the directness of his appeal. They felt that they were listening to one who, with courage and independence of mind, had faced the issues for himself and who spoke out, without flinching, the truth to which he had fought his way. Step by step he led them along the path which he had found firm under his own feet. He inspired them with the confidence which a climber feels in a strong young guide. Other ways up the mountain there might be, but this he had found and knew. Along it, steadily and cheerfully, he led those who followed him and who, as they followed, learned to trust his strength of character and his knowledge of the ground.

Character, said Goethe, makes character. Spirit kindles spirit. Thought with life and courage in it makes those who come under its influence more real in their thinking and braver in their quest of the truth. Lectures like these leave the mind ashamed of lingering among half-beliefs. They impel it to a decision. That decision, be what it may, each one, with such help as he can find, must make for himself. In the making of it there is a moral factor as well as an intellectual. These lectures help towards the strengthening of both. They are infectious with courage. And they bid us, in the grounding of belief, put out to the full our powers of accurate sight and of just reason, while training both under the guidance of those who can teach us how to see and how to draw conclusions from things seen. This, in the different fields of its application, is the discipline and method of science. And these lectures claim that, in the scientific study of the evidences of the Christian Faith, the thinker must be sensitive to the facts of spiritual experience, observing them truthfully, sifting them patiently, and reviewing them in the light of the corporate tradition of the Christian Church, ' the blessed company of all faithful people.'

M. E. SADLER.

January 5, 1910.

THE FAITH
AND MODERN THOUGHT

LECTURE I

THE GROUNDS OF OUR BELIEF IN GOD

I WISH to begin this course by calling
attention to the vastness of the subject which
both to-day and in the ensuing lectures we are
to consider. It seemed to me best, when I
received the invitation of the Executive to
give these lectures, that we should try to
adopt some one point of view and follow it
out as far as possible over the whole field. In
doing that I am very anxious not to suggest
that other points of view are to be regarded
as less valuable. It is very improbable that
we shall all of us find it most natural to
approach the subject from exactly the same
standpoint. I have adopted one which I

THE FAITH
AND MODERN THOUGHT

LECTURE I

THE GROUNDS OF OUR BELIEF IN GOD

I WISH to begin this course by calling attention to the vastness of the subject which both to-day and in the ensuing lectures we are to consider. It seemed to me best, when I received the invitation of the Executive to give these lectures, that we should try to adopt some one point of view and follow it out as far as possible over the whole field. In doing that I am very anxious not to suggest that other points of view are to be regarded as less valuable. It is very improbable that we shall all of us find it most natural to approach the subject from exactly the same standpoint. I have adopted one which I

B

believe to be the best for this particular
purpose; and it seems to me well to try to
make the lectures a coherent whole by following out one point of view, rather than to
make them scrappy and disconnected through
attempting to approach the subject from
various points of view, though each of these
may be legitimate and valuable.

A word must therefore be said about the
method of the whole inquiry. The method I
wish to adopt is, so far as I understand it, the
method of any scientific procedure. I suppose
everybody here knows that no science exists
which quite conforms to what the logic text-
books call deductive and inductive methods.
Those things are possibly useful, certainly
fictitious. All thinking proceeds by bringing
together general principles, which have been
reached as the result of past experience, and
all the new facts bearing upon the subject
which can be found; and I am hoping to show
that we always, as a matter of fact, set out
with a certain ideal of knowledge before us,
namely a coherent and comprehensive statement of the whole field of fact; but that coherence at any rate is a demand which comes

solely from reason, for we have no ground in experience, so far as I know, for insisting that the world shall be regarded as coherent, as all hanging together and making up one system. But we do demand it. And I am further to show that, as our knowledge stands at the present moment, this ideal of reason and the facts of experience stand over against one another in hopeless and irreconcilable antagonism, unless all the essential points of the whole of dogmatic Christianity are true : that is to say, if you like to put it so, that Christian theology is the only hypothesis that meets all the facts. That is what I shall try to show.

To-day we are to begin with the question of the ground of our belief in God ; and I must say immediately that, in one sense, this is the subject of all the lectures, because, as we proceed, we shall, I hope, be making clearer to ourselves what we mean by the word 'God.' It is not enough to prove that some sort of Being exists. In the end, the only thing that matters is the character of that Being. But to-day it must be enough that we shall to our own intellectual satisfaction (and no other satisfaction is in question at these lectures) establish, if that may be, the existence of a Governing Will, from which the whole Universe proceeds and upon which it all depends.

Now the first evidence to the religious man of the existence of God is his own religious experience. No one who has had even a moment of such experience can afterwards quite ignore it; it will perpetually challenge his attention. He may, of course, find great difficulty in combining the fact which he seemed then to reach with all the other established facts of science and everyday life. It remains there as a problem; and as evidence it always has this peculiar perplexity about it, that it is incommunicable. If another man says, " I have not the faintest idea what you mean when you talk about communion with God," how can we explain it to him? And if he then goes on and says, " Moreover, how are we to be sure that this experience of yours was not due to self-hypnotism? May it not very well be the case, that you had this experience, whatever it may have been, because you expected to have it, and your imagination worked at the command of your expectation, or else because you were in the company of a large number of other people who were liable to this peculiar disorder, as it may be, of the mental faculties?" How is one to answer that? Suppose he still goes on and says, "Besides, there is no evidence apart from your experience that this Being, with whom you have met, exists at all. It is possible to explain all you tell us simply by referring it to morbid psychology and pathology. There is no fact there for you to apprehend." And what shall the religious man say? When these two considerations are both before us, the incommunicability of the experience itself, and the apparent absence of any independent ground for believing that the "fact" which we reached in that experience exists at all, don't we feel as if the whole foundation of our religious life were exceedingly precarious? Most of us, I think, have been disturbed by that charge of self-hypnotism. How can we disprove it? Don't we feel very much as the old Psalmist felt when he was kept away from the Temple services?—"Like as the hart desireth the water-brooks : so longeth my soul after

Thee O God. My soul is athirst for God, yea, even for the living God : when shall I come to appear before the presence of God? My tears have been my meat day and night; while they say daily unto me, Where is now thy God?"

It is to meet that state of mind, if we can, that these lectures have been arranged. For there are some who, though they have been in touch with what is spiritual, have felt compelled by motives which we must respect, by reverence for truth, to believe that it was all illusion; while others have never come in touch with what is spiritual at all, because the intellectual barrier has always stood in the way and prevented them from yielding themselves to the influences. That means that religious experience appeals for external support. It is not enough for it in the mind of a scientific man that it happened to him, that the man should have had such and such feelings, such and such momentary convictions; if that is all that is to be said, morbid psychology is the science to which the study of this experience belongs. We want some evidence, apart from the religious experience altogether, that the God whom we reach in that experience is really existent. And this makes a peculiar feature of the whole of theology, or of the science of religion. All the other sciences at least assume the existence of their subject matter. The physicist is not called upon to prove that mechanical forces exist. The geometrician is not called upon to prove there is such a thing as space. He is allowed to assume it and no one quarrels with him. But when the theologian begins to try to develop a theory of the world on the basis of this experience, he is at once challenged with the question: How do you know that this experience is really a valid guide to fact? And that question must first be answered, because it is undoubtedly true that some people have very little or even none at all of this specifically religious experience.

But may I say immediately that by religious experience I do not mean an ecstasy or an extraordinary thing that happens to a few people here and there, but simply that impulse, which comes upon most people at some time, to throw oneself back upon a Power greater than oneself, and the sense, the perfectly sure sense, that that Power has received one and is supporting one. Numbers of people have felt something of that sort. It is a sense of self-abandonment and yet of safety; and that seems to demand, as I have said, further support from outside; and that support must be of a rigidly scientific character : nothing else will do.

Now it has often been suggested that we shall find an end of our difficulties if we consider the chief of scientific principles, the principle of Causation. As we all know, science consists mainly in the attempt to find causal relations, and to "explain" events by referring them to their causes. The scientist does not usually trouble himself as to what Causation is, and he generally does not know: but that does not matter. We are then told sometimes that whatever is a cause is always also an effect of a previous cause; but that this cannot go on for ever; and there must be a first Cause; something must have started the whole series. I believe that contention to be essentially true, but that this way of putting it is quite unsound. For the life of me I cannot understand why it should not have gone on forever. I see no reason why you should suddenly introduce a First Cause in that chain of reasoning backwards that is carried on in the natural sciences : for example, when you have traced back the Solar System to the Nebula, science is not going to be content to say that this was produced by a first Cause ; it is going to try to find out what was the origin of the Nebula, if it can. It may not succeed in finding out; but that will not prevent science from believing there is an origin to be found if a man of sufficient capacity ever arises or if the necessary evidence is forthcoming. No one is content, then, at any given point to introduce the notion of a First Cause. But that means, that wherever the effort is made to employ that argument, science will reject it. We shall never find God simply by tracing the world back and back through the process of its development and looking for its starting point. Science will not allow us a starting point at all.

But I think there is more to be hoped for from another method. Science makes one colossal assumption always ; science always assumes that the world is rational in this sense, that when you have thought out thoroughly the implications of your experience, the result is fact. The scientists who have produced the electrical theory of matter believe that the result of their scientific inquiry is the fact; that the chairs and tables of our ordinary use consist not only of molecules, which consists of atoms, but that even the atoms themselves are each a kind of Solar System of centres of electrical force. Well, they do not look like it : and yet that is believed : it is believed on the sheer evidence of reason. You are assuming that when you have thought accurately about the facts of perception, the result of all that thinking is fact equally with the thing you first perceived. That is the basis of all science; it is a colossal assumption, but science cannot move one step without it. That means that a rational coherence is assumed by science as running right through all our experience. It is all assumed to fit together in a rational scheme, whose principles we can· discover if we have the necessary power of thought. But then one may take a step further, which natural science is not required to take for its own purpose, but which we are required to take if we want to understand all the facts, and not only physical or only chemical facts. Our knowledge is just as much a fact as anything else. My knowledge of the existence of the table is quite as much a fact as the table is. My knowledge, then, is one of the facts which must be held together in this coherent scheme. Now that seems to involve, as far as I can understand the position we have reached, that there is some mentality (I know no better word for the purpose) in all the facts of our experience. I do not mean to say that the chairs and tables are thinking; I mean that everything which exists must be the embodiment of rational principle. The Universe turns out to be a rational whole. Now that is an enormous result. Remember where we started from. Science begins with its demand that that world shall be seen as coherent; it insists on looking at it, on investigating it, till it is so seen. As long as there is any phenomenon left out of the systematic coherence that you have discovered, science is discontented and insists that either the system is wrongly or imperfectly conceived or else the facts have not been correctly observed.

I know no better statement of this part of our problem than what Mr. Balfour said in his Presidential Address to the British Association in 1904. He had been speaking about the electrical theory of matter and how it seems to reach a real unity and to reduce to a single principle all physical facts; and he continues : " Whether indeed this vehement sentiment in favour of a simple universe has any theoretical justification, I will not venture to pronounce. There is no *a priori* reason that I know of for expecting that the material world should be a modification of a single medium, rather than a composite structure built out of sixty or seventy elementary substances, eternal and eternally different. Why then should we feel content with the first hypothesis and not with the second ? Yet so it is. Men of science have always been restive under the multiplication of entities . . . Nor for my part do I think such instincts should be ignored. John Mill, if I rightly remember, was contemptuous of those

who saw any difficulty in accepting the
doctrine of " action at a distance." So far as
observation and experiment can tell us, bodies
do actually influence each other at a distance ;
and why should they not ? Why seek to go
behind experience in obedience to some
a priori sentiment for which no argument can
be adduced ? So reasoned Mill, and to his
reasoning I see no reply. Nevertheless, we
cannot forget that it was to Faraday's obstinate
disbelief in " action at a distance " that we
owe some of the crucial discoveries on which
both our electric industries, and the electric
theory of matter, are ultimately founded.
While at this very moment physicists, however baffled in the quest for an explanation of
gravity, refuse altogether to content themselves
with the belief, so satisfying to Mill, that it is
a simple and inexplicable property of masses
acting on each other across space . . . Now
and again it happens that observation and
experiment are not treated as guides to be
meekly followed, but as witnesses to be broken
down in cross-examination. Their plain message is disbelieved, and the investigating
judge does not pause until a confession in

harmony with his preconceived ideas has, if
possible, been wrung from their reluctant
evidence."

Why ? Simply because it is more satisfying
to the intellect. Here then is this colossal
assumption, that the truth about facts is what
satisfies the mind of man : that is the basis of
all science.

Now this seems already to give us a kinship
between the mind of man and the Universe he
lives in.   It does not take us far yet ; it does
not give us yet a living God. We have found
no principle of will or purpose there as yet.
All we have found is that science, whose
method is surely justified by its results,
always assumes in the real world the existence
of those principles which govern our thinking.
And now we go on to a point which science
for its own purpose is not called upon to
consider.   Science investigates our experience
and tries to discover the origin of the present
condition of the world, the process by which
it has arisen ; and it calls that discovery the
" explanation " of the present fact.   Yet it is
never satisfying to the mind altogether,
because it takes the world piecemeal.   It

takes to-day and explains it by yesterday. But take to-day and yesterday together, and ask—Why these two ? Science will go back further to the day before ; but take the whole series together—why this series and not another ? There is still that question to be asked, to which no answer, apparently, is forthcoming. The mind, which in its scientific procedure is assuming that its logical or intellectual satisfaction is the guarantee of truth, is still unsatisfied before this long history, which only connects one event with another, and never tells us why the whole series of events should be this and no other ; and many people at any rate have raised that question concerning the whole world as they see it.

"Oh Love ! could you and I with Him conspire
To grasp this sorry Scheme of Things entire,
Would not we shatter it to bits—and then
Remould it nearer to the Heart's Desire !"

We shall not have done with this problem till the end of our course, and yet the fact that there is a problem of evil at all to the human mind shews that the mere tracing of history, which is all that natural science has ever professed to do, will never produce intellectual satisfaction, and therefore, by the admission of Science itself, will never produce final and ultimate truth. Now there is in our own experience already one principle which does answer the question, " Why ? " in such a way as to raise no further questions ; that is, the principle of Purpose. Let us take a very simple illustration. Across many of the hills in Cumberland the way from one village to another is marked by white stones placed at short intervals. We may easily imagine a simple-minded person asking how they came there, or what natural law could account for their lying in that position ; and the physical antecedents of the fact—the geological history of the stones and the physiological structure of the men who moved them—give no answer. As soon, however, as we hear that men placed them so, to guide wayfarers in the mist or in the night, our minds are satisfied. And speaking generally, the moment we agree with anyone that a thing is good it never occurs to us to ask why it should exist. There is no problem of the existence of good. Purpose is a principle which we have already gauged in our own experience and which, where it is applicable, gives a final answer to the question Why ; and there is no other principle known, at any rate to me, that does give a final answer to the question, Why.   We have already seen that the principle of Causation in the ordinary sense does not.   It can only state facts of history, and you may always say, Why this history ?   The only principle then that will satisfy the scientific demand for complete intellectual satisfaction is the principle of Purpose ; science requires, therefore, that there should be a real Purpose in the world.[1] Grant that, and the whole of our experience, as it seems to me, immediately begins to become coherent.   Of course the problem of Evil remains : why was the Purpose this which we see and not another ?   That for the moment we shall leave, but we shall come back to it in the subsequent lectures.   But surely it is scientific, when you already have a principle capable of explaining the fact, at

---

[1] N.B.—This is not the argument from Design, which does not deal with the world as a whole, but rests on the adaptation of one part to another part.

least to investigate and see what can be done with that principle. It is not as though we had to invent the term "Purpose" to explain the fact of the world, as the old scientists invented Caloric to explain the fact of heat. Purpose exists in our everyday experience. It supplies an answer to our question. It is then scientific to accept that answer provisionally as a hypothesis.

I believe that the effort to understand this Purpose is not so hopeless as it looks at first. Scientific principle requires us at least to take seriously the hypothesis of a Purpose in the world, and, therefore, a real Will behind the world. That hypothesis will not be justified until we have seen it through, until we see how it does as a matter of fact cover all the facts and particularly the fact of Evil. And let me say here that to declare the problem of Evil insoluble is Atheism or Agnosticism. The problem of Evil must be soluble. The Revelation of God in Christ exists to be the solution. Whether or not we shall be able to grasp that solution in a single course of lectures—or in our whole life-time—is of course another question. Yet I think we may get clearer about it than perhaps we have been before.

But now, leaving the further development of this thought of the Purpose that is in the world, let us go back to our starting point, which was religious experience.

These two seem now to support each other. For what is the leading characteristic of the religious experience? Surely it is this : that in it the man is in contact with a Being who appears to know him through and through, who is intimate with him as no human being is, and yet whose knowledge is not felt to be intrusive or in any sense a vexation. We might feel that it was an intrusion if some even of our friends had the faculty of knowing all our inmost thoughts, however much we tried to keep them to ourselves; we should probably resent it ; and people do resent that claim when it is made. Nobody ever dreams of resenting the thought that God knows him through and through. He may tremble at the thought, but he does not resent it. Now what Being is there who could conceivably know me in this way, a Being other than my-self, who yet has an absolute knowledge of

everything that goes on in my innermost
nature? Only one possible Being, surely: the
Being who made me. He might know; no
one else, as far as I can see, could know. If
there is a Being who made us, He might have
such knowledge.[1]

It seems, then, that the two sides of the
argument are beginning to support each other.
It appears from the investigation of science,
from investigation of the method of scientific
procedure itself, that there must be a Will in
which the whole world is rooted and grounded;
and that we and all other things proceed
therefrom; because only so is there even a
hope of attaining the intellectual satisfaction
for which science is a quest. And here is an
experience, very common among men, which
claims to be a direct contact or communion
with a Being, Who, if He exist at all, must be
the Maker at least of the man who has the
experience; and if we already believe, on quite
other grounds, that there is such a Being exist-
ing, it is surely the very height of presumption
to say that the man who believes that he is
in communion with that Being is deceived,

---

[1] Cf. Coleridge's Poem, γνῶθι σεαυτόν.

simply on the ground that we perhaps have not had a similar experience. If it can be shown that God exists, then there can be no objection in principle to the thought of His revealing Himself directly to the individual. The difficulty about the religious experience was not any doubt in the man's mind as to whether he had it or not : he knew he had it ; he knew that this extraordinary event had taken place in his life ; but the difficulty was that so many other people had not had it, and at first there was no evidence for the existence of the Being whom he then perceived ; he remembered how under various influences people may perceive things which have no real existence ; and he wondered whether he himself was the victim of such a pathological condition.   But when he has found that the most rigid investigation of experience that can be made leads to the hypothesis of a creative Will which is the root of all existence, then he says, " Now I have proved that what I then perceived does really exist.   Other people may be blind to it : that does not affect my vision ; I have seen it."   And so it seems to me the demand of Reason and the religious experience

support one another ; either without the other
would be precarious. The demand of Reason
by itself would set up an ideal to be reached,
which yet nobody had reached. It would say
that there must be somewhere the Creative
Will; but would still admit that no one has
in any way ever perceived it. And on the
other side the religious experience is precarious
in the way that we have shown ; but the two
together support each other ; the intellect demands the existence of such a Being, and if so,
then agnosticism, (if by that we mean anything
more than the reverent confession of our own
intellectual failure to understand completely
the Object of our religious worship), is not
scientific ; it is precisely a refusal to apply the
scientific method itself beyond a certain point,
and that a point at which there is no reason in
heaven or earth to stop. The way in which
it arises, I think, is simply that people become
so much occupied with the consideration of
what they know, that they entirely forget the
perfectly astounding fact that they know it. It
is by considering the fact of knowledge itself
and what is involved in knowledge, namely,
this astounding demand of the intellect that

experience shall be made to appear coherent
and so forth—it is by considering these facts
that we are led on to the further principle,
which lies outside the field of natural science
no doubt, but is yet reached by the application
of the strictly scientific method.

And then, if all that is true, it will follow
that the course of the wise man will be to
study with all his power the character of that
Will and Purpose which governs the world;
he will wish in every way he can to increase
his knowledge of this subject, for upon that
everything else depends: and recognising,
moreover, that this Power is almighty, since
all proceeds from it, it will be his wisdom,
unless indeed the Power shall turn out to be
definitely evil, to ally himself with it as far
as he may, and to cultivate the faculty of
communion with it—a faculty that can be
either cultivated or stunted. And then, too,
as he comes to understand the character of
that Purpose, he will try to apply it in his
own life, not only from the strictly religious
motive, but also from the strictly scientific
motive, for he will want to verify his
hypothesis: he will say, "The hypothesis

is that God exists, and has such and such
a character : let me live in the light of that
hypothesis and see what happens; let me
make experiment with it in the one place
I can, in my own life. Possibly, as the old
theologians used to say, I must believe in
order that I may understand. I cannot
believe unless I understand a little; but I
shall not understand much, unless I am
willing at first to take a certain amount
on trust and make experiment with it: and
that experiment must be made in myself,
because my will is the only will that I
can bring, or begin to bring, into harmony
with the divine Will. It is only in my own
person that I can try to discover what alliance
with the divine Will means." And so the
scientific and the religious impulses will
combine, and will lead a man to submit
himself and all his powers to the God in
whom his reason has led him to believe.

REVELATION AND FAITH

IN the last lecture I tried to show some of the
reasons why, not only as persons upon whom
God has in a measure poured out His spirit, but
simply as rational beings, we ought to believe
in God; and that, not only in the sense of
acquiescence in the theory of His existence,
but of trust in His Wisdom and Power.   I suggested that our religious experience (by which
I meant, not some remote and strange ecstasy,
that may have fallen at times upon a few
outstanding individuals, but our own religious
experience which I venture to think all of us
have had in some degree) is in itself, as far as
it goes, evidence for the Being of God : but
that from its very nature it always demands
further support, because it may be suggested,
either by others or by our own experience in

other parts of our life, that all this is hallucination and self-deception; and therefore we
need to be assured that, apart from the experience which we seem to ourselves to have
of the Divine, the Divine really exists as fact;
and we find that support by investigating the
impulse which lies at the root of all scientific
procedure, the impulse to grasp the world as
an intellectually satisfactory whole, seeing
how all the parts are connected together by
intelligible principles. And then, we said,
the mere fact that the world does correspond
in this way to our intellectual demand calls
for explanation, and, further, the world as a
whole, the entire series of events in time, calls
for an explanation which the methods of
natural Science cannot give because they
do not deal with that type of question at all.
The methods of science explain one event by
reference to other events; they explain the
facts of to-day by reference to the facts of
yesterday, and so on : when you take the
whole series of yesterday and to-day together,
and ask, Why this and nothing else ?—there
is no explanation possible, except in terms
of purpose: that is to say, the scientific

demand that the world shall correspond to the method of our intellect, the scientific demand for an intellectually satisfactory world, can only be satisfied by belief in a Purpose running through the whole, a Purpose rooted, as all purpose must be, in Will. Then we came back to our starting point and said, this experience of a Power in whose hands we are, seems precisely to correspond with such a Will, for its leading characteristics were, that we are altogether in the hands of this Power, and that this Power is intimate with us and with our own inmost thoughts as no other human being can be, as only the Maker of souls could be. Consequently we found that this hypothesis of a Divine Will, which seemed necessary to justify the method of Science itself, is confirmed by our religious experience, and our religious experience supported by it. The two together make an intelligible scheme of things. And let me say again that by this religious experience I mean that sense that we all have of a Power about us encompassing us and guiding us, by which we are all upheld.

All of us have felt that in the particular

form which I suggested in the last lecture,
that of throwing ourselves back in times of
distress or perplexity on a Power which
receives and supports us.   There come those
times in the lives of all, I think, who have to
make critical decisions ; the man simply
abandons himself absolutely and whole-heart-
edly to something, he hardly knows what,
and the abandonment is justified.   He finds
himself not, as it were, falling aimlessly through
an abyss, but supported and carried on to
something perhaps better than he had dreamed
of.   Very often, at least, that has happened in
greater or less matters, I expect, to all of us,
certainly to very nearly all.   That is our
basis and our starting point ; and it is of that
type of experience that I wish to speak more
especially in this lecture ; for that type of
experience is what, in its culminating forms,
we call Inspiration.   It is the awareness of
the Presence of " a Power not ourselves."
Sometimes that awareness, that sense of God,
is very dim and has hardly any content, and
is simply the sense of a Power ; but that
same experience in its most vivid form is
what we call Inspiration, when the man can

say "The Word of the Lord came unto me saying."

Let me preface what I have to say to-day about Revelation with these verses from the Book of Exodus:

"And Moses said, Shew me, I pray thee, Thy glory.   And He said, I will make all My goodness pass before thee; and I will proclaim the name of the Lord before thee, and I will be gracious to whom I will be gracious, and will shew mercy on whom I will shew mercy. And He said, thou canst not see My face: for man shall not see Me and live.   And the Lord said, Behold there is a place by Me and thou shalt stand upon the rock; and it shall come to pass, while My glory passeth by, that I will put thee in a cleft of the rock, and will cover thee with My hand until I have passed by; and I will take away Mine hand and thou shalt see My back; but My face shall not be seen." [1]

And I would preface what I have to say about faith by reminding you of the words of Job,—"Though He slay me, yet will I trust in Him." [2]

[1] Exodus xxx., 18—23 (R. V.)   [2] Job. xiii., 15.

And now, how shall we distinguish the form of knowledge that we arrive at through Inspiration from other knowledge? In the first place I think we should remember that all knowledge comes from God, because He is the ground of everything that exists at all, and therefore of our knowledge. If we know, it is only because He has given us the faculty of knowing; it is through Him and from Him that we have any knowledge at all. And also all knowledge is directly or indirectly knowledge of Him and His method; for He is the Maker of all the world; His is the Purpose which we see manifest in all the facts of life; and therefore, as we study those facts, we study the product of His will. As we study what He has made, we must come to know something about Him who made it. All knowledge, then, comes from God, and all knowledge is at least indirectly knowledge of God. But there is a very great difference between the knowledge which is the conclusion of a long train of reasoning and the knowledge of direct acquaintance. We can hardly believe in God at all without admitting that our knowledge comes from Him and tells us about Him.   But there remains a great difference between the philosopher and the prophet.   The philosopher arrives at his view of the nature of God and of the requirements of God by thinking and arguing ; and he says at the end,—" Therefore we see that the will of God is so and so."   The prophet says,—" The word of the Lord came unto me saying, Thus saith the Lord."   There is all the difference in the world between the two.   The mark, we said, of the religious experience is that we find something : something is there before us, presented to us : we do not argue about it, we meet it ; and in its supreme form, prophecy, where the man is in so intimate a relation with the object of his experience that it seems actually to take the place of his own thinking and to tell him what he shall say, we have the climax of this type of experience in which we do not argue to God but find Him : and I wish to insist that this not only gives the prophet a confidence and power over men which no philosophical argument can give, but it provides something of a wholly different kind, because always, when we think, we end up with generalities.   All philosophy culminates with the Divine; only religious experience can give us God. We all know the difference between a picture and a description of a picture. The description is all in general terms; perhaps there is only one picture in the world to which all those terms together are applicable. It still remains true that the words do not call up before us the actual picture. No description can take the place of the picture itself. Or think again of any acquaintance of your own and how hopeless a task it is really to describe him to someone who does not know him; all the words remain generalities; they may be true enough; but they never give the friend to whom you are speaking a real knowledge of the third person. Always it is by direct experience, and only by direct experience, that we understand individuals; and this is true not only of individual persons but of individual things. Consequently, for religion, philosophy is always a mere introduction, to some people an unnecessary introduction; they do not want it at all; to others a necessary and inevitable one, but always only an introduction. At the end there comes the meeting

with God, which is always God's revelation of
Himself; for we cannot suppose at this time
of day, if we believe in a God at all, that it is
possible for a man to surprise His secrets ; we
cannot suppose that we are going to know
anything about God either against, or even
without, His will.   All we know will be what
He likes to tell us, what He is pleased to show
us ; that is all.

But this direct experience which is of
inestimable value for religion, (for in fact
without it religion cannot exist at all), is none
the less always conditioned through and
through by the character of the person who
has it.   All our experience, even our
perception of ordinary physical objects, is
conditioned by our capacity to perceive.   You
may put a geranium in flower in front of
a colour-blind man, and he won't see the
difference between the flower and the leaves ;
it is there, but he cannot see it ; he has
not the necessary faculty.   So in the case of
any artistic object; whether or not we
appreciate a really beautiful object depends
mainly upon our own capacity in relation
to that kind of object.   We have to train our

perceptive powers and our capacity for appreciation. People always like rather bad art at first. It requires some training, some intimacy with pictures, or music, or whatever it may be, to enable us to like the things which the experts go on telling us are the things that deserve to be liked. And again with our friends, I do not argue myself into liking a man; certainly not: but whether I like him or not depends on two things,—what I am, and what he seems to me to be. I shall not like people of a certain type because of my own temperament; they won't be congenial. But also what they seem to me to be will depend upon the kind of person I am. If I am generous I shall think they are too; also if I am niggardly; if I am suspicious I shall suppose they are always suspecting me; if I have any courage I shall not easily credit them with cowardice; but if I am cowardly I shall always be looking for some hidden terror by which to account for their most heroic actions. We all know that. It depends upon ourselves how much of other people we are able to see when they are there before us.

Most of all is this true in man's relation with God. God may be before a man in all the beauty of holiness, and the man not be able to understand it, not have the faculties for perceiving it. And that is how it is that in the beginning of the Revelation everything is crude, a great deal is even wrong; not because God has deceived the man, but because the man has not yet the faculty for understanding. Men do not understand God without trouble any more than they understand human beings or pictures ; indeed much less, inasmuch as the subject itself is much greater. And so we shall expect to find that God's revelation of Himself, as it is recorded, is always conditioned by the capacity and circumstances of the people to whom it is given. At first man simply trusts to God because there is nothing else to trust to, and He attributes to God the qualities that he most admires. In the early ages when a man is merely a member of his tribe, and hardly an individual at all, he attributes to God the leading characteristic of his tribe. And then gradually, in his intercourse with God, his own capacity to perceive and to understand will grow, and his vision of God, the unchanging God, will become clearer and clearer.

There was one people who came out of the East, the home of religion; who dwelt for a time in Egypt; who then went and inhabited a ridge of hills and a few plains in the very meeting-point of the East and the West; who were then carried away from their home, that there might be nothing national left about them except their religion, and who came back held together by religion and by nothing else; until all the elements of religious life could come to flower in a single human Personality. The Jews are forever the specialists of the human race in religion. Greece gave us philosophy and art, Rome gave us law and social organization; Palestine gave us religion; and the record can never be obsolete. In the early ages the nations of the world were specialists in their respective departments. We shall never again, probably, have quite the same purity of intellectual interest as the Greeks; very probably we shall never have the same capacity for ideal sculpture as the Greeks; because their temperament ran to this expression and all the circumstances of their life pressed out in those directions. Every impulse of Greece was concentrated upon art and every impulse among the Jews was concentrated on religion ; and that is not likely to happen again.   They remain the classical expression of the distinctively religious temperament.   But there is progress in revelation.   At first, understanding God's zeal for Israel, they did not equally understand His equal zeal for all other nations ; and Deborah could pronounce a blessing upon Jael the wife of Heber the Kenite as if that were the whole of Divine truth in the matter ; and Elijah could confidently massacre four hundred and fifty prophets of Baal to celebrate the victory of Jehovah on Mount Carmel.   And people point these things out and ask—"How can you say this is the revelation of God ?"   The answer is—Look at the book as a whole.   Can you anywhere find anything like that record of persistent growth in the understanding of the Divine ?   Must you not say, these men from the beginning to the end were in intimate communion with God ?   Nothing else can account for what you find there—the steady growth of spiritual insight from the naïve religious nationalism of the early days, until Amos proclaimed God's sole sovereignty, and Hosea learnt something of the tenderness of His love, and Isaiah upheld his righteousness as the standard of political and public life, and Jeremiah learnt something of the secret of suffering, and Ezekiel taught the responsibility of every individual soul before God, and the great Prophet of the Exile, who wrote the latter half of our book of Isaiah, discovered something of the Divine redemptive suffering. Nowhere else will you find this steady growth in the understanding of the nature of God, and it is impossible that that growth should have gone on, unless the Divine had been present to that people's mind as it has scarcely been to any nation since then, so that they might go on seeing more of its truth and beauty, and recording faithfully what they saw. As has been well said, "We should treat the Bible not as an inspired record but rather as the record of inspired men": and we go to school with the Biblical authors, not to think what they thought, but to learn from them how to think ourselves.

The principle of "authority" is not the authority of someone imposing upon us beliefs from without, but the authority of a man who has had experience such as we have not had, probably, in an equal degree ; but we can learn from him more about it.   The art student, who goes to Italy to learn in the school of the great Italian painters, does not intend to do nothing else but paint reproductions of their pictures all his life ; but he knows he will never be able to paint modern subjects properly, he will never be able to solve modern artistic problems properly, unless he trains himself under those old Masters who had such absolute control of their own emotions and their own expressions.   Just so I would suggest that we should go back to the inspired men of the past, not to find a short cut to truth, (there is none), but to find out how to find truth.   These men were in contact with the Divine.   We can learn something of how their conception of the Divine grew in their own minds, and we can learn by what steps they established their communion with the Divine, so that following their example we may establish our own.

For this inspiration is never — never — a guarantee of truth. Just remember what the view of the Israelites themselves was upon the subject. In the Book of Deuteronomy [1] there are several tests given, by which it may be proved whether or not a prophet is false; and we are inclined to think at first that by "false prophet" is meant an impostor, a man who claimed inspiration that he had not got. But remember the story of Micaiah the son of Imlah, as he stood before Ahab and set about to explain how Ahab's prophets had called upon him to go up to Ramoth-Gilead, and he said, "Therefore hear the word of the Lord: I saw the Lord sitting upon His throne, and all the host of Heaven standing by Him on His right hand and on His left. And the Lord said, Who shall entice Ahab, that he may go up and fall at Ramoth-Gilead? And one said on this manner, and another said on that manner. And there came forth a spirit, and stood before the Lord and said, I will entice him. And the Lord said unto him, Wherewith? And he said, I will go forth and will be a lying spirit in the mouth of all his

[1] *e.g.* Deut. xiii. 1—5.

prophets.   And the Lord said, Thou shalt entice him, and shalt prevail also ; go forth, and do so.   Now therefore, behold, the Lord hath put a lying spirit in the mouth of all these thy prophets, and the Lord hath spoken evil concerning thee." [1]

Now however you regard that incident, whether you think that Micaiah is relating a vision he has really had or is throwing into the form of a vision his own belief about the facts, it is clear that Micaiah believed in the possibility of false inspiration, and also that the people to whom he spoke believed it too, for to suppose that Micaiah at that moment uttered what was popularly regarded as blasphemous is to credit him with a quite impossible blunder.   And now there is this extraordinary statement of Ezekiel : " And if the prophet be deceived and speaketh a word, *I the Lord have deceived that prophet*, and I will stretch out my hand upon him, and will destroy him from the midst of my people Israel." [2]

What does this mean ?   It means surely that the prophet is so certain that in his moment of inspiration God has spoken to him, that

_____
[1] I. Kings xxii. 19—23.   (R. V.)   [2] Ezekiel, xiv. 9.

when another man comes and says, "God spoke to me, too," the prophet does not call that in question; what he calls in question is the truth of the message given him. On the whole it must have seemed to them of more vital import to maintain that men were in genuine communion with God than to insist that in communion with God we apprehend the truth. And in all the ages of open vision it is thought necessary to test the import of a vision before it is believed. Just compare the cases of Saint Theresa and others in the mediæval Church; the vision comes, but before the import is accepted various tests are always applied. Wherever this experience is frequent, people refuse to believe the content of the prophetic message, if there is nothing more to be said for it than that it came in an abnormal sort of way. The content must shew itself to be true. May not the solution of the problem really be found in what we said just now about our only perceiving what we ourselves are qualified to perceive? God is there, always the same, always truth, always righteousness; but the men who have been trained, as the prophets were trained in the schools of the " sons of the prophets," to bring themselves into communion with the Divine can still only appreciate what they are fit to appreciate ; they will still always, as we all must, see God through human eyes ; and it is only the pure in heart who see Him truly. The others will see something, they will see a distorted vision ; and no one is quite perfectly pure in heart.   Consequently we shall expect to find, what we do find, gradual development and steady progress among the inspired men.

What that leads us to, I think, is this ; that in inspiration we are given, not solutions, but new data ; we do not get the solution to a problem that was puzzling our minds ; we get a new fact altogether ; we find a new element in the Divine.   The new data may not suggest a solution of the old problem ; they may make it, for the time being, apparently more insoluble than ever : but always what you get in inspiration is not doctrine but fulness of life.   It is contact with God ; not understanding of God, but living in vital union with Him : and it is possible that the man who has the most vital communion with God will be least able to make a scientific theory of that experience. I suppose that Shakespeare knew very much less about the method on which he constructed his plays than either Coleridge or Professor Bradley. It is possible to be a great artist and a bad critic, a noble character and a bad moralist. It is possible to be a great saint and a bad theologian. And very likely it will be true that the people who have the greatest capacity for arriving at the true theory of the religious experience will not be the people who have had the supreme blessing of that experience themselves. A man may see a flash of lightning and account for it by saying that the cloud was broken and he saw light behind, thinking it was sunlight. That would be a bad account of the matter; he may then come to the man of science who had not seen the flash of lightning but can give a correct theory of it after hearing the fact described. Just so, it is not always the inspired man who gives us true doctrine, but often someone who comes afterwards and supplies the theory of the facts which inspired the man. Through inspiration we get the facts, the data, of the religious life; if you like, we get religion

itself; but not theology—and while we are
bound to go to school with the inspired men
for our religion, we are not bound to accept
their theology.   Indeed, unless we are to suppose that the work of the Holy Spirit upon
the mind of man has already come to an end,
we may expect that theology, that is to say
doctrine, will go on growing and progressing
as long as the church exists.

This, then, I think, should be our attitude
to that part of God's revelation of Himself
which is given in inspiration.   We should not
in any sense try to silence our intellects; but
we should say,—Here are the great facts of
religious history; here are the facts which any
true account of the matter has got to include
and be just to; and any crude, rough-and-
ready rationalism which leaves out those facts,
or leaves them unaccounted for, or calls them
hallucination, is thereby self-condemned.
They are the most important facts in life.
But still we may say, that the man who found
the facts may not perhaps have found a theory.
Let me give a crucial instance.   There is no
record in the Church of a more prolonged and
more effectual communion of a man with God

than that of St. Paul. Any theology which
does not rest upon the Pauline experience of
God and Christ is condemned at once ; it has
left out the greatest appreciation of the fact
which we have. But we may still say, surely
we must say, that St. Paul was endeavouring,
so far as he was theological, to account for
that experience in the terms which were current
at the time, which the people to whom he
wrote used and could understand ; and they
were not really adequate ; and we can still go
back to the same experience and see whether,
with all the other growth of our knowledge,
we could give a better account of the matter
than he. We cannot move a step without
him ; our theology, if it leaves him out, becomes vapid and vacant ; but our theology
need not on that account be his.

What then is that faith, which is our
answer to revelation ? and what is our faith
in general ? All our life is based on faith
of some sort. In science, so far as we apply
the results of our science, we rest upon a
faith, (for it is nothing else), that the laws of
nature will be to-morrow what they are to-day.
There is no reason to the contrary ; but there

is no reason for saying they will be. Yet we believe it, and we trust implicitly to that hypothesis, and our trust is justified in practice. In practical life we do the same. If we are ill we consult a physician, and we don't refuse to take his medicine until he has proved to us that it will do us good, or shown how it will do us good. If our financial affairs are embarrassed we talk to a lawyer and take his advice; we don't demand that we shall understand all the intricacies of finance; we trust him. So here, surely, if there are men who are experts in religion, (and that is what inspired men are), it is but sanity to trust them. That does not mean believing all their theories; it does mean taking them as our guide in this region; we remember that what they supply is data, and not they only, for their vivid form of communion with God is something we too have in our degree; and our main object in going back to them is to learn by contact with them how we may increase our own sense of communion with God. To begin with, we trust the saints. That is always the order. We are told about

God, and we believe what we are told. We believe first what men tell us ; our faith does not at first rest, as a rule, upon any direct apprehension of God. As children we were told about God and we believed what we were told. And then gradually, as we acted on that belief, experience came in our own lives, experience which, with most of us, has steadily grown, although there may have been great interruptions from one cause or another, sometimes moral causes and sometimes intellectual ; but that experience has steadily grown until we believe no longer because of what others told us but because we have tried to live the life they suggested and we have found that the experiment has worked ; we have the basis of faith in ourselves.

At first, in the history of the race, faith is very desperate, like Job's, " Though He slay me, yet will I trust in Him." Man clings to God, not because He has shown Himself trustworthy, but because there is nothing else to cling to ; we are altogether in His hands, let us hope He means our good. And then that trust begins to justify itself. At first, no doubt, the conception is very crude; there is just a dim sense of a vague Power, and the man will take any material object that he comes across and treat that as the embodiment of God; this is the "fetish" stage in which a man will beat his god or dress him in bright calico, according as he treats the man well or ill. All that, though so crude and remote, is the beginning and the germ of what comes later. And then there comes a great epoch in religion, the rise of deliberate idolatry, where the god is conceived of as an individual being, and therefore in only one place at a time : there is a sanctuary, a shrine, for the god, and men resort to the god who is beginning to have some real character in their conception of him. Then there comes the stage when the idol is discredited. As the conception of God becomes more spiritual and transcendental, idolatry is given up. But that leads to something rather remote and abstract. In the Jewish Holy of Holies there was no image, but there was an empty space which was the figure of the Unfigurable, and it reminded men, precisely by contrast with the idols of the surrounding

E

nations, that God cannot be represented in any limited form because He is Infinite. Thus gradually God became exalted, but also, for most men, became rather remote, and the process of redemption itself became almost a disappearance of all our sin in the purity of God, symbolised by the sacrificial smoke which rose in a thick cloud from the Temple court to vanish in the purity of God's heaven: "I have blotted out, as a thick cloud, thy transgressions, and, as a cloud, thy sin."[1]

And then we arrive at the final stage of revelation. The prophet always presents God in human form; he speaks of the arm of the Lord, of His hand, of His wrath, of His love; and our trust in God, if it is to be real, must alway be trust in a God who appears in human form; and the greatest epoch of religion and of faith would be already come if there is in history a manifestation of God in concrete embodiment,—an embodiment not in stone or any dead matter, but in living manhood, which will have the whole power of the statue, and more than the whole power of

[1] Isaiah xliv. 22.

the statue, over the imagination, and yet never check the freedom of the spirit. For it is not when God is thought of as something other than man that we adore Him most ; we must indeed adore the Holy One that inhabiteth Eternity ; but the perception that we must adore Him is almost purely logical. We understand it ; but we do not feel it. We shall never feel the necessity of adoration until we have seen God manifest in a life comparable in its mode with our own, because it is just the comparison that brings us to our knees. It is when God is most human that He is most unmistakably divine.

That leads us on to the subject of our next lecture, the discussion of our need for the occurrence of such a Life. But meanwhile when all this revelation comes upon us and we have in our degree responded to it in faith, that faith must issue necessarily in worship. Now worship will always have two sides, a practical side, in our conduct, for our whole life will become an act of worship ; but worship must also have its own life in adoration, in prayer, and in communion. And I wish, while we are still dealing with this part of our subject, to say something about each of these.

Adoration is the natural response of man to the sense of the greatness of God, and it is the easiest of all forms of worship. Where it predominates, the tendency, I suppose, is usually to what some would call a " catholic " type of worship, where there is a solemn rite, and a consecrated priest standing between the worshipper and the exalted God ; and though in some sense all creation shows forth the glory of God, yet some elements are to be consecrated as the actual vehicles of His Presence, hallowed for that purpose, because only after such an act can we dare to believe that the exalted and transcendent God is verily before us. The danger here is always Quietism, the danger lest we think that since God is so great we cannot really serve Him, and all we have to do is to bow before Him and gaze upon His beauty. And yet if He is great through love, we can serve Him ; for love needs answering love.

Then there is the life of worship in prayer. Here the most vivid sense, I suppose, is that of God always ready to help, always about us,

encompassing us with His love, and ready to
give whatever is good for us : and where this
sense is predominant we find the " evangelical "
type of worship, where no intermediary is
permitted between man and the God who loves
him, and no places are set apart specifically
for God's worship ; for all good work is consecrated and may be conducted in God's House.
And the danger here is always lest we suppose
that in prayer we are suggesting to the
Almighty something that He had not thought
of or was unwilling to do.   And it is quite
clear that both dangers—the danger of isolated
adoration and the danger of isolated prayer—
will be met, precisely in so far as the two are
practised together.   The man who adores
before he prays will be in no danger of thinking
that what he has to do is to press some course
of action on Almighty God.   But then arises
the question : Why pray ?   Well, surely,
because God is always waiting to give us all
the things that are good for us ; but whether
they are good for us will very likely depend
upon whether we recognise that they come
from Him.   For example, victory over temptation is, no doubt, a good thing in itself:

but suppose that a man wins a victory over temptation, acting, as he thinks, entirely in his own strength, and becomes in consequence morally self-confident and forgetful of God— possibly it would have been better for him that the temptation should have continued. But if he has first fully recognised that all good things come from God alone, then that victory will become good.   There are things which are good only when we recognise the source from which all good things must come ; and the most natural and obvious way of expressing our sense that only God can give us these blessings and our desire to receive them, is to go to Him and to ask.   But, of course, every Christian prayer, at least, contains explicitly or implicitly the petition—"Not my will but Thine be done," expressed by the words we add to our prayers when we say that we ask through Christ, or in His name, or for His sake.   It is only if He too desires what we have prayed for that we want it. And so the essence of prayer is not, of course, the moving of God's will by ours—(a blasphemous and wholly ludicrous conception, for, since God is infinite in Wisdom and Love no addition to His good-will towards us or to

His knowledge of our need is possible), but the bringing of our will into dependence upon and conformity with God's, in order that the blessing He is waiting to give may really bless us, and so He may be able to give it.[1]

And all this will culminate in Communion, where the worshipper blots himself out and merges himself in the whole body that God may be all in all, as in adoration he strives to do ; and where he receives into himself the Divine life that in all things he may live by the Spirit of God as in prayer he strives to do. The two come together there. And if our communion is to be perfect, it must be communion with God manifest in human form ; for it must be a union of spirits in love ; and it is only with other men that we can be united, with beings we can understand, who are like ourselves. God Himself must appear before us as infinitely loving according to our understanding of love, and not in some remote philosophical sense, if our communion is to be perfect.

So these are our conclusions for to-day. Our religion rests upon the religious experience

---

[1] Since human nature is essentially social and the human race is spiritually one, prayer may be vicarious, and is then called intercession.

of ourselves and of the holy men of God.
We go always to those holy men to develop
our own religious capacity, not simply to
think their thoughts, which were to make it a
form of idleness, but to learn from them how
to think our own thoughts, how **we** too,
according to the capacity God has given us,
may be in as intimate relation with God as
they were according to the capacity He gave
them. And then, as we learn in this way, we
surrender ourselves to Him in faith, expressing
that faith through adoration, prayer and
communion. All of this is the most evidently
rational thing in life; to ignore this, to depart
from this way of life, is simply to fly in the
face of an immense record of experience of
the most vital facts in the world; but we see
too that, while revelation is always limited by
our capacity, while as was said to Moses we
can, as it were, only see the Lord after He has
passed by, and never gaze immediately upon
His Face, yet if God is to be revealed up to
the limits of our capacity, if we are to trust up
to the limits of our capacity, if we are to
worship up to the limits of our capacity, God
must Himself appear before us in human form.

LECTURE III

THE HISTORIC BASIS OF CHRISTIANITY [1]

TO-DAY we are to discuss the historical evidence for the fact of Jesus Christ, and first of all we have to ask, why do we need this fact? We need it for two reasons; one is psychological, the other is logical and philosophical. We need it, first of all, because a truth which is embodied in a story and in a person has far more effect upon our minds and wills than a truth which is only stated in abstract propositions. One needs something upon which the imagination can fasten, something which can sway the affections, something which can change the will; and no doctrine can do any of these things, as was discovered long enough ago. The intellect by itself has no motive force; it cannot by itself supply ideals, or at least, the kind of ideal that really moves us. We can think out

[1] For the historical parts of this lecture I am much indebted to my colleague, the Rev. B. H. Streeter.

an ideal we already have, or we can think out
the way to realise an ideal which we have
already formed, but we cannot set ourselves
in motion by mere thinking. Mere intellect
has no motive force. And then, too, it is
always the case that the forces which sway us
most are those which appeal to the deepest
rooted and most primitive impulses. There
is an eloquent passage in Mr. Graham Wallas'
book on *Human Nature in Politics*, where
he deals with this subject and shows how it
may have happened to a man once in a
thousand years to be privileged to stand and
listen while Pericles abstracts from the million
individual Athenians what it is that gives
Athens its meaning for the world, " but
afterwards all that he will remember may be
the cadence of Pericles' voice, the movement
of his hand or the sobbing of some mother of
the dead." [1] And that, I think, represents
what all of us have experienced at one time or
another. The thing that really stirs us may,
perhaps, have to be rational, because if our
reason rebels against it we shall resist; but it
must be also more than rational; it must be

[1] *Op. cit.* p. 73.

something that can appeal to the emotions; and it is necessary, therefore, if the revelation of God is to have its full hold upon us, that in the eternal Divine utterance there should be some dominating gesture, that the Word should become flesh for our hands to handle.

We need the fact of Christ, then, psychologically, because we are so constituted that if truth is to have full weight for us it must first be embodied.   But won't a myth do this just as well as a history ?   It may be urged that a great dramatist gives us figures every bit as individual, every bit as moving, as any of the figures in history, and perhaps more so, because he has spent time and trouble upon perfecting the character he draws, and he is not fettered by considerations of fact. He can make the picture as perfect as he pleases, and as effective as he pleases.   But it is not true that a myth will do as well as history for this reason, that what we need of the particular fact in question is that it shall be to us the revelation of the Eternal and Almighty God.   Now in the moment when we are under the fascination or spell of the story it may not matter to us whether it is true or not ; we are carried away and we act. But at other times, which are after all the most frequent times, we must justify this trust to our intellects ; we must have some sure platform of belief on which we can stand when the moment of inspiration is not present. And if that is to be so, we must not only feel at certain times an intense admiration and reverence for Christ, but we must be persuaded that Christ is the revelation of the Divine Power ; we must be persuaded that the secret of life is revealed there.

Now if we think of God either as the indwelling Principle of the world, or, more adequately, as the Will, the Almighty Will, upon which all existence depends, then it concerns us more than anything else to know the character of that Will ; and if the story which claims to be the revelation of that Will is a myth we shall have to say—Where is the evidence that God is like that? This is a beautiful drama, no doubt ; yet where is the evidence that we see here the secret of life? But if in very truth the Life of Christ was lived, then we say, the principle which issued there must be adequate to that manifestation of itself. It cannot be a mere blind force; that does not explain anything: it must be adequate to what it has done. If the root principle of reality has blossomed once in so exquisite a flower that is new evidence as to the nature of the plant. Thus psychologically, and philosophically also, we need the fact of Christ if we are to believe in the love of God. All the revelation that we were considering last time is unable to defend itself against the suggestion that it at least may be hallucination. No one indeed can prove that it is; and we may even say that in all probability it is trustworthy, if we have already established the existence of a Divine Will. But how are we to prove that this experience of ours or of anybody else is really communion with the Divine Will? We need something more objective, something in the world of fact to which we can turn and say, This has happened; and by whatever principle you explain the world, that principle must be adequate to this occurrence, and must have in it the power to produce such an achievement. Logically, therefore, as well as psychologically, we need the fact of Christ, if our belief in the love of God and His revelation of Himself to us is to be rationally defensible and morally effective.

So then we ask what is the evidence ? Primarily, without question, the existence of the Church. How in the world are you to suppose the Church came into an existence, unless Christ is a historic person ? You must have some starting-point for this enormous network of ecclesiastical organisations ; you must have a foundation which is adequate to the fact. And the Church's theory of its own foundation is adequate. Indeed, the difficulty really is that the foundation seems more than adequate to the fact ; for it seems easy to ask and difficult to answer, why the Divine Founder should found an institution so remote in .its practice from His own ideals. But at least it is true that the Church's theory is adequate. The Church says that it was founded by a historic Figure whose spiritual pre-eminence is such that we cannot but confess Him the revelation of God in human life. That is adequate. And how else are you going to explain the fact of the

Church ? For, remember, however far short the Church may have fallen at times from its own ideal, it has always represented and stood for an ideal not to be accounted for by the ordinary social environment of the times. Perpetually, of course, the influence of the world has told upon it and dragged it down ; but it still remains true that the principle which it has upheld, the principle which breaks out in the moment of the Church's own degradation and revives it over and over again in history, is a principle not to be discovered in, or accounted for by, the ordinary social influences of the time. This is something perfectly intelligible if the whole Church is rooted in a Divine Christ who is also a historical figure : otherwise it is not intelligible at all. And keeping in our minds the thought that we have somehow to find an explanation for the Church's existence, we may go on to the difficulty of the imperfection of the Church. And I think it need not take us very long ; for we see that if the Founder's purpose is to produce a type of character and to achieve a spiritual result, then the new force which he brings into the world must take men as it finds them, and win their free consent, never forcing their minds or wills, never compelling them, but winning from them free allegiance, and securing acceptance always because it is seen to be good, and never by the exercise of any over-ruling and over-powering authority. But if that is true, then, of course, we shall expect the whole history of the Church to be one long conflict between the ordinary worldly nature of the men who make up the body of the Church and the new spirit which is the Church's real life.

And now let us proceed to those documents in which the Church enshrines its own record of its own foundation. We are dealing, you will remember, simply and solely with questions of evidence and not at all at present with questions of edification. As a matter of evidence the first thing we have to do is to be quite clear what points are contained in the first three Gospels and what in the fourth, and to exclude the fourth. If the facts contained in the first three Gospels are established, then perhaps we can go to the fourth Gospel for the interpretation of those

facts. The religious value of the fourth Gospel is quite incalculable; but it is not evidence; at any rate in the present state of the controversy it is not evidence, because a very large number of the most sincere critics are unable to determine that it is the work of an eye-witness, or even that the writer himself supposes the events to have occurred precisely as he tells us. We shall come back to the fourth Gospel next time, but as long as the critics are disputing about its authorship, as they are now, it is not fair to use it as evidence. What are we to say, then, about the other three Gospels?

Now I will begin rather late, because there are certain wild theories current which suggest that, the moment you let yourself into the snares of Biblical criticism, you will find yourself compelled to believe that the Gospels are a fabrication of the second or third century. Where that myth comes from I have not the remotest idea, but it exists in various people's minds. Now about the year 180 A.D. you have Irenæus; and Irenæus is already so certain that there are four authoritative Gospels and only four that he begins to

prove *a priori* that it must be so. But
nobody begins to prove that such and such
must be the case, until he at any rate is sure
that it is so ; and this reflection is made more
interesting by the further consideration that
Irenæus' arguments are quite indescribably
bad ; one is the argument that there must be
four Gospels because there are four winds and
four corners of the Earth, and so on. So
confident is he that there are four and only
four that he is prepared to argue like that.
By 180 A.D., then, at latest, there was no
doubt that there were four official Gospels.
Again, not later than 170 A.D. you have
Tatian composing what he calls the Diates-
saron, the harmony of the four Gospels, which
shows that in his time too there were four and
only four official Gospels. Before that you
have Justin Martyr about 160 A.D. certainly
using our four Gospels. In 140 A.D. the
heretic Marcion produced a mutilated version
of St. Luke, showing that St. Luke was then
already an authority. But what is perhaps
most important for our purpose is this, that
Papias, who was already Bishop of Hieropolis
in 120, so that he cannot have been a very

young man at that time, mentions that the Elder (his authority, and perhaps the author of the fourth Gospel) said that Matthew wrote the Logia (we shall come back to what the Logia were in a moment), and that Mark, who was the interpreter of Peter, wrote what he remembered of Peter's teaching accurately but not quite in order.

Now if you take the first and third Gospels and bracket off, say with blue ink, every section that is contained in both of these and also in St. Mark, you find in the first place that it is the greater part of St. Mark, and that it is a great part of the first and the third Gospels.   And if you then bracket off, say in red ink, all the rest of the first and third Gospels that are common to those two, you will find that it is a considerable proportion of the remainder, and consists entirely of teaching. The obvious inference, an inference accepted with slight modifications by all the critics, is that the first and third Gospels, St. Matthew and St. Luke, rest upon the second Gospel and another document now lost ; that in composing the first and third of our Gospels the authors had before them previous evidence

F 2

which they used : St. Mark was a part of it and this other document was another part. Now, as we saw, we have got to give all the four Gospels time to become fully official before the date of Tatian ; and such a process takes some time.   We also have considerable evidence in St. Matthew that some of the first generation of disciples were still alive when it was written, for it contains many promises that the Second Coming will be before that generation has altogether passed away.   Then St Luke's Gospel we now know to have been written by St Luke.   The evidence that has lately been accumulated for that view is quite overwhelming.   It is chiefly linguistic, show- ing that the Gospel and the whole of the Acts are by the same author as those parts of the Acts where the author uses the words " We " —" we sailed," " we fetched a compass," and so on ; all these are by one author, St. Luke. Now St. Luke met with St. Paul about 52 A.D., and obviously was then a fully grown man. You have then to put the third Gospel in the lifetime of someone who was a fully grown man in about 50 A.D.   That brings you again within the first century.   Now St. Matthew and St. Luke in the first century, writing as far as we can tell in wholly different atmospheres, for wholly different sets of circumstances, yet find that both St. Mark and this other document are already established authorities and base their Gospels upon them; that leads to a very early date for these two documents.

Now what is the character of this other document, which we will call Q, the name nearly always given to it from its German title " Die zweite Quelle," the Second Source? What is the character of Q, and what is its date?   Its date is such, apparently, that it was already an authority even when St. Mark wrote.   There is a very large amount of evidence that St. Mark used it, particularly in the fact that the document itself consists almost entirely of teaching.   Now St. Mark uses the words that represent teaching, either the verb or the noun, more often than either St. Luke or St. Matthew,[1] and in proportion to the length of the Gospel a great

---

[1] διδαχή—Mt. 3, Mk. 5, Lk. 1.   διδάσκω—Mt. 14, Mk. 17, Lk. 17.   See Hawkins *Horae Synopticae*, p. 10.   Sir John Hawkins has kindly pointed out to me that the verb διδάσκω is used of our Lord *in narrative* Mt. 7, Mk. 13. Lk. 10 times; this of course strengthens the argument above; c.f. especially Mk. x. 1 (ὡς εἰώθει) and vi., 34.

deal more often ; and yet he hardly gives any
of it ; with the exception of the 13th chapter,
which is an entire critical problem by itself,
there is hardly any discourse of our Lord in
St. Mark's Gospel and yet St. Mark is always
referring to His teaching. Surely this implies
that the Lord's teaching was already known.
Not only is this the case, but St. Mark
appears definitely to use this other document
on several occasions. I will mention three,
which anyone can refer to, as about the most
obvious, the preaching of St. John the Baptist,
the story of the Temptation, and the incident
when our Lord's enemies accused Him of
working miracles in the power of Beelzebub ;
in all these cases, if you look at them, you
will find that the account in St. Matthew and
St. Luke is longer than that in St. Mark.
Now unless we are going to throw up
altogether the hypothesis of the two documents as the basis of St. Matthew and
St. Luke, we shall have to say that St. Mark
here alludes, for instance, to the Temptation ;
he knows it is far too important an event
to be left on one side, but he does not give
the whole story because people already have

that in their hands; and similarly with the other incidents : it is not necessary to do more than to speak of them as facts; the details are already known. There are a large number of detailed instances that anyone who studies the Gospels very carefully, looking out for traces of this, will discover, where St. Mark abridges the account of the incidents given in full in the other documents ; and this, of course, is further evidence that this document was already an authority at the time when St. Mark was writing, and shows that his many allusions to our Lord's teaching refer to this document either alone or among others.

And now we go further; what is the character of the document Q from which our record of the teaching is derived ? It appears to be a production of the primitive Palestinian Church. It is impossible here to do justice to the arguments which lead to that conclusion, and, rather than weaken them by compression, I will refer to Mr. Streeter's essay on *The Literary Evolution of the Gospels* in the volume edited by Dr. Sanday and entitled *Studies in the Synoptic Problem.*[1]

[1] Clarendon Press.

We can quite understand that the early
Church would be anxious to record as soon
as possible the sayings of the Lord. Nobody
was going to forget how he went about healing men of all manner of bodily and spiritual
diseases; nobody was going to forget the
story of the Last Supper, of the Betrayal, of
the Crucifixion, of the Resurrection : these
things need not be written down, there is no
fear of their perishing at present. But we
must write down His teaching at once because
words are so easily forgotten. And there was
a danger, a danger whose reality the fourth
Gospel proves, that their homeliness and terse-
ness would be overlaid. The teaching must
be recorded at once ; and this document, used
by our first and third evangelists, goes right
back to the very beginnings of the whole
Church, so that it would become a manual of
teaching that missionaries could leave behind
them as they went on their journeys, when
they had persuaded the people to accept
Christ as the Lord of life. If the converts said,
"Now what do we do in consequence of our
acceptance of Christ as Lord ? " the preacher
could hand them the Teaching of the Lord

and say, "Do your best to live up to that standard." And then later on we find again what we should expect; as the disciples, the personal disciples, of the Lord were disappearing from the earth and there seemed to be none left who actually remembered the events, we find a demand for a written narrative, and when St. Peter himself is martyred at Rome, the people come to St. Peter's interpreter, St. Mark, and beg of him to write down at once, before he forgets it, all he can remember of the chief-of-the-Apostles's teaching : and so you get St. Mark's Gospel, which, differing absolutely from Q in this respect, contains almost nothing but events, and lays the whole emphasis upon the Passion. The whole book is a "story of the Passion with an introduction," whereas Q seems to have contained no account of the Passion at all. In St. Mark everything is centred upon the Passion; the last week takes up a third of the whole Gospel. Since those early days St. Paul had brought out the true significance of the Cross of Christ; in the interval between the first document and the second document, the whole Gospel of the Cross of Christ had come into

being and its meaning had become known.
Everyone now saw that everything turns
upon the Crucifixion and the Resurrection;
and so that becomes the pivot of the whole
Gospel. Thus we reach a result, which as far
as I can see is absolutely established; St.
Mark gives us in his Gospel, written whilst
St. Peter's teaching is fresh in his mind,
and wholly based upon St. Peter's own
evidence, the record of the outward frame-
work, as it were, of the Lord's life, and besides
this we have a document giving us the teaching of the Lord which goes back to the very
earliest ages of the Church.

Thus we begin with this certain datum of
the moral and spiritual ideal upheld and
realised. We begin with evidence as good as
anybody can demand for the teaching of our
Lord, for the ideal He set before people and
for His own realisation of it. Compare the
Sermon on the Mount with His own behaviour
before Caiaphas and Pilate. He not only
conceived an ideal but He realised it; and
that is our certain datum: a moral and
spiritual ideal upheld and realised. And
then there come the two other evangelists.

It is very difficult to determine the authorship of the first Gospel, but criticism seems
inclined to think it impossible that it should
have been written by St. Matthew. On the
other hand, there is every reason to suppose
that St. Matthew was the author of the other
document which both the third and the first
Gospels use: for Papias' memory was, that
he was told by the Elder, how Matthew wrote
the Logia or Utterances of the Lord. Well
then, if a Gospel is composed, part of which is
St. Mark's and nearly all the rest of which is
St. Matthew's, there is no difficulty in explaining how St. Matthew's name came to stand at
the head of it, because anyone can see what in
it belongs to St. Mark ; and the rest is actually
St. Matthew's. St. Luke tells us definitely in
his preface that he took great trouble to find
the various records and to test them and sift
them ; he has a large amount of special
information, more indeed than St. Matthew
has ; several of the longer parables, Dives and
Lazarus, The Unjust Steward, The Good
Samaritan, The Prodigal Son, are in St. Luke
and St. Luke only ; but we can be sure from
his preface that he has been at great pains to

test his sources. It is useless, as far as I can see, to speculate as to where he may have found the record of these parables or anything else that is peculiar to him, although an obvious source is suggested by the story of how he and St. Paul stayed together with St. Philip on St. Paul's last journey to Jerusalem.

Here, then, is our starting point,—a moral and spiritual ideal upheld and realised. But that is not enough. It is not enough that the governing Power of the world should once have produced this great instance of spiritual pre-eminence; for it is, after all, just possible that it was produced only to perish, and that the Almighty Power had no more interest in this being than in any other being. That would still be just possible. Perhaps you remember the end of Thomas Hardy's novel *Tess*,—"The President of the Immortals had finished with Tess." If all we have yet stated were the whole story, we might say at the end, "the President of the Immortals had finished with Christ." If we are to be on sure ground in taking Him as the revelation of the Divine, it is necessary that the Divine Power should be seen clearly co-operating with Him, carrying Him through His ultimate self-surrender, and bringing Him out victorious. We need the Resurrection.

What, then, is the evidence for the Resurrection? Here again the chief evidence is the Church. Somehow or other we have to account for the fact that the Church came into being. European history, at least, from that day to this has been mainly the story of interaction between the Church and the-outside world. We must find some ground for this great fact; and to attribute it to hallucination is to reduce the whole of European history to a perfectly insoluble enigma. If we believe in the Government of the World by the Divine Will, we shall not acquiesce in the belief that the Church with all its beneficent activities is grounded on a hallucination. Moreover, to attribute the Resurrection appearances to hallucination is psychologically outrageous. The disciples were plainly not in a state of mind that could produce hallucination. At the Betrayal they all forsook Him and fled; many of them were probably already well on their way back to Galilee at the time of the Crucifixion.

There they were, the scattered followers of a discredited Messiah; and suddenly they became the nucleus of the greatest political achievement of the human race. Something has got to happen; and it cannot happen simply in their minds, for they are not going to become convinced for no reason whatever that the Lord is alive; the thing is out of the question. The only conceivable explanation of the gathering together of the Apostles as the nucleus of the Christian Church is that Christ was actually alive and in communion with His friends. There is nothing else that can possibly account for that fact; and if that fact is unaccountable, then history from that day to this is unaccountable. Unless we are prepared to give up all efforts to think scientifically and to find causes for events, we must see that what these people believed was that Christ was in communion with them again as really as He had ever been; and this belief could only arise if the fact were so. And then we go to the documents with that thought in our minds. First we have St. Paul's evidence: the list of appearances given in I. Cor. XV. is plainly a traditional official list,

—an official list already extant and accepted by 56 A.D. at the latest. Then we pass on to the Gospels. Well, of course I know that anybody who likes can show that it is difficult, perhaps impossible, to bring out any consistent chronology in the Gospel-records of this period. But why rationalistically minded folk should suppose that in a moment of almost intolerable joy people are going to have an exact memory for dates and places I cannot conceive. Of course there are inconsistences in the story; it would be monstrous to demand anything else; but what stands out all through is that time and again they were convinced of the presence of the Lord amongst them as they cannot have been convinced unless He was there. And then, following upon that, there is the story of the empty tomb and the risen Body. It all fits in; it all harmonises. We may find it difficult to understand it, or to picture to ourselves exactly what it was that happened. I do not know why we should very much wish to do so; for religious purposes, what matters is that the Lord was alive. As far as I can see it does not matter very much what became of His Body. I do

not doubt that His Body was in some way
risen and glorified; but if anybody finds this
incredible, that need not prevent him from
believing in the reality of the Lord's Resurrection. That the Lord was alive seems to
me certain.

There then is our basis historically. We
have the first and third Gospels within the
first century. We have them already taking
St. Mark and another document as authorities,
and when we examine St. Mark and that
other document we find that St. Mark brings
us back to the memory of St. Peter himself;
and the other document goes back to the
primitive Church and the beginning of all
things; the evidence is as good as can possibly
be desired. Sometimes it is asked why there
are not more records or allusions bearing upon
these documents in early Christian literature?
Chiefly because there is hardly any such
literature. Just think of how much of it
there is—the letters of St. Ignatius, one letter
of St. Polycarp, one of St. Clement of Rome,
the spurious Epistle of Barnabas, the Shepherd
of Hermas and the Didache—and they are all
of them documents in which it would be

impossible that there should be many allusions to contemporary Christian literature ; and yet, even there, we find quotations and references, though, of course, not very many. The objection, then, that is raised to these early dates for the authoritative documents, seems quite negligible, and the early date itself seems to be the only one that is the least compatible with the facts.

And so we have all the facts we require established, and we are able to say confidently that the efforts to explain the story of Christ by any other means than the theory of the Church about its own origin in His historic Person are all of them thoroughly unscientific. They try to account for facts by causes which will not account for them. They try to account for the Church by principles which in no way explain its power in the world even if they explain its bare existence ; and particularly with reference to the Resurrection they have to suppose hallucination on the part of the disciples in circumstances where hallucination is absolutely out of the question. To refer so great a factor in human history as the Church to an event which cannot possibly have occurred is, to say the least of it, unscientific.

We have said nothing about the character of our Lord's teaching, or about His own realisation of it, beyond pointing to the fact that He did realise His own ideal. To all of that we shall come next time ; and we shall find that, if we agree, as we must agree, that the Spirit of the Universe is for us expressed in human language in the Person of Christ and that the secret of life is there revealed and made manifest, this will involve for us no mere basking in the sunshine of Divine favour, but rather our entrance into the spirit of a life whose historic occurrence is amply demonstrated, whose moral and spiritual pre-eminence consists in the completeness of self-sacrifice, and whose inspiration for those who try to imitate it is without parallel in human experience.

LECTURE IV

In the last lecture we established, if I carried you with me, the fact of Christ. To-day we are to consider the nature and significance of that fact; and the difficulties, which have beset us hitherto in this course of lectures, become in this connection almost overwhelming. In the first place there is the difficulty that people approach the subject from very different points of view; and we must agree, that, if Christ is what the Church has always claimed that He is, no one individual and no group of individuals can possibly exhaust His significance. The unsearchable riches of Christ are not to be possessed by any one man; they belong to the Church. For that reason it is very likely to appear to many that anyone who speaks on this subject from a particular point of view is beginning altogether at the wrong end. And another difficulty is that our interest in the subject is due to its sanctity; and thus we are involved in the problem, to what extent we should allow the emotion of reverence to colour our treatment. There will be some, to whom it will appear that the influence of that emotion can only obscure the clear process of the intellect: and there will be others to whom a purely intellectual treatment seems profane.

Perhaps, after all, the subject itself will carry us through; for our task is to understand the Lord, so far as may be in a single hour, as He appeared to the people among whom He lived; we are to go back, if that may be, behind all the theology, behind our own worship and adoration, to the historical fact, and try to see what the outward form of the Lord's life was. It was through appreciating that outward manifestation that the first disciples reached their theological position and commenced their life-long devotion. And for us, too, it cannot be anything but-healthy to go back to that basal fact and study it, if we can, for a time apart from the theological significance that we attach to it ; and then come again to the question : What is the meaning and value of the fact that we have apprehended ? For there is a great danger that our confession of our own limitations will end, in effect, by imposing upon the Lord our own conceptions of what He should be. We all agree that we shall not find the whole truth about Him for ourselves, and that other men may have found parts of the truth which seem hidden from us ; but the moment that admission is made, there is great danger that we shall be content simply to set up our own ideal independently and read it into the life of Christ. We must go back to the actual historical fact and find out how the Lord appeared among men, and start from there.

And first I would call attention to the unparalleled completeness of His religious life. There are two strands in our religious life which are very rarely combined, in any degree of fulness, in the same person ; they seem to be almost incompatible with each other There is the ecstatic, fervid type which appears in the prophet, who is appallingly aware of the importance of moral choice, and who is aware, with a vividness that is nearly always painful, of the presence of God and of His purity and holiness. In almost all the great mystics we find that curious combination of a longing for a return of the mystical experience with a memory that whenever it has come it has been more intensely painful than anything else ; but it is upon the stormy immediacy of their experience that I would lay stress. That is one type, the ecstatic type. On the other side we have the quiet, calm confidence of firmly established faith, when a man fears nothing because he has put his trust in God, and is content to leave all great issues in God's hands. One of the paradoxes of religion is that both these elements must be present in some degree. It is vital to a complete religion that it should insist upon the responsibility of man before God ; and it is quite equally vital that it should insist that all our lives are in His hand. How those two are to be reconciled is one of the great problems of religion of which perhaps I may say something in the last lecture ; but we cannot deal with it now.: What we have to observe is that in all human religion one or other of these tendencies predominates, and it is quite clear to which type any given man belongs. In the case of our Lord there is endless dispute as to which type can claim Him. Various writers have brought out different sides. Perhaps our first impression is that indicated by Harnack when he says that the "most astonishing and greatest fact about Him" is that "entrusted with the greatest of all missions, His eye and ear are open to every impression of the life around Him—a proof of intense calm and absolute certainty." [1] He watches the sower as he sows his seed : He observes the beauty of the lilies ; He calls the children to Him in the street. That is one side ; and it is quite true ; His confidence in the power of God is absolute,—not one sparrow falls on the ground without the Father. [2] But there is another side ; the moment after the baptism, that is, so far as we can tell, the moment that He became convinced of His own Messiahship, the Spirit drove Him into the wilderness

[1] *What is Christianity ?* p. 36.   [2] Mt. x. 29.

to be tempted of the devil.[1] And it was
possible for men to say that He was in
league with Beelzebub;[2] and His own
relatives, too, said,—" He is beside Himself."[3]
There is all the directness and vividness of the
ecstatic type of religious experience; both types
are here in absolute fulness. Writers of the
one temperament emphasise His calm, and
His repose; writers of another temperament
emphasise the prophetic and ecstatic nature of
the ministry. Both are there in full development; and yet, surely it is true to say that the
element of confidence is the stronger; that He
never for one moment in all those times of
storm and stress doubted the omnipotence or
the love of the Father; that He emerges even
from the Agony in the Garden prepared for
the scene before Caiaphas and Pilate.

We may take another instance. Some
writers exalt Him as wholly different from
other men; some wish to insist that He was
just as other men, going about among them,
a man among men. Are not both true? He
was the friend of ordinary people. He was
the welcome guest at a wedding feast; He was
no stern ascetic. It was a possible libel to

---

[1] Mk. i. 12; Mt. iv. 1.   [2] Mk. iii. 22.   [3] Mk. iii. 21.

say that He was a gluttonous man and a wine-bibber.[1] And yet, all through, He is absolutely alone.   The disciples never understood Him until after He was withdrawn.   At the end they all forsook Him and fled : and we see Him in His absolute loneliness as He bears the Cross.   But that loneliness is only the climax of the whole life from the beginning ; He is in spirit quite alone ; He alone knows the secret of His mission.

Now there is one problem which we must consider, because I think it is the problem which has caused most trouble to careful students of the Gospel story in recent times ; I mean the question that concerns our Lord's apocalyptic utterances about His own Second Coming. Certainly the Early Church expected His return almost immediately, of that there is no doubt ; and it is recorded that He spoke of His own return as something immediately about to happen. It used to be the fashion to attribute all this to the misunderstanding of the disciples, to suppose that they had misrepresented the Lord's sayings. Lately the tendeney has rather been to accept these sayings as genuine ; and even Dr. Sanday, certainly a

---

[1] Mt. xi. 19.

cautious, and certainly an orthodox writer, has used the phrase that in reading the prophecies of the Lord we have "to determine, not only what the Son meant, but what the Father meant, speaking through the Son." [1]   That is, we must be prepared to think that He was mistaken as to the mode of the inauguration of His Kingdom.   And upon that foundation has been built up a very strong attack upon His whole ethical teaching ; it is pointed out that, if He was expecting the end of the present Dispensation almost at once, His indifference to all worldly goods and possessions, and the " counsels of perfection " in the Sermon on the Mount may have had their root in this misapprehension.   And I see no way of completely answering that charge if we accept this suggestion that He did actually expect His own immediate return. Yet it is certainly true that to refer all these sayings merely to the misunderstanding of the disciples is unscientific and uncritical.   Once we leave our sources, we can spin no end of cob-webs about what we suppose the Lord to have said. But there is one saying of an apocalyptic kind

---

[1] *The Life of Christ in Recent Research*, p. 118.

which seems to me to give the clue to our problem. When the Seventy returned and reported that they had the same power which the Lord Himself possessed over what in those days was called possession by devils, He replies, " I beheld Satan as lightning fall from heaven."[1] Surely the meaning is clear. The report comes that His spirit is working through His disciples ; it is leavening the world ; and in the beginning of the process He already grasps the end ; the power which can defeat the power of evil is there ; and in the beginning of its work He sees the final over-throw of evil : in the moment of strong excite-ment His imagination bodies forth before Him the triumph of His cause, and He says,—" I beheld Satan as lightning fall from heaven." With that clue we go on to the sayings about the end " of this age." They are all connected apparently with the Fall of Jerusalem. We know how our Lord had yearned over Jerus-alem all through His ministry. " O Jerusalem, Jerusalem, how often would I have gathered thy children together, and ye would not."[2] Jerusalem was the embodiment not only of His

[1] Lk. x. 18.　　[2] Mk. xxiii. 37

people's hope, and at first certainly of His own
hope, but of everything that stood for oppo-
sition to His cause, for spiritual self-content-
ment and comfortableness and deadness, which
was the real enemy He had to fight.   And so,
as He looks at the city which thus represents
the whole of the opposing force, and as He sees
the necessity of its downfall, in the collapse of
that last barrier He grasps the whole triumph
of the Kingdom that shall follow.   I think you
will find if you study the apocalyptic writings
generally, that they come from a type of
religious genius which apprehends as it were
in a single moment what must take centuries
to work itself out, and what is known by the
Seer to need centuries to work itself out.   So
here the Lord sees in the vision of a moment
the triumph of His Kingdom ; but He knows
quite well that it is not coming all at once.
" The Kingdom of God cometh not with observation." [1]   " So is the Kingdom of God, as if
a man should cast seed into the ground ; and
should sleep, and rise night and day, and the
seed should spring and grow up, he knoweth
not how." [2]   There is much to show that in

[1] Lk. xvii. 20.   [2] Mk. iv. 27.

our Lord's conception the growth of the Kingdom was to be gradual. It is even very likely
true that it was precisely this conception of the
growth of the Kingdom as against its sudden
descent from heaven which so much perplexed
the minds of His hearers in Galilee, excited as
they must have been by the apocalyptic conception of the Messianic Kingdom of which
the air was then full.[1] That is why the Parables seemed to them so obscure;[2] for the
" word " which " the sower " scatters is the
proclamation of the Kingdom ; the comparison
of this to a seed which may or may not grow
would be unintelligible to people accustomed
to the vivid language of apocalypse. All this
language of apocalypse He will use at times
of great crisis to emphasise the decisiveness of
certain events in the history of the Kingdom.
But at other times, when He has calmly set
forth the principles on which it is to grow, He
shows that He intended that it should be, as
it has been, a gradual steady growth, not a

---

[1] A complete study of this and kindred subjects would have
to include a discussion of the contemporary apocalyptic
literature—such as *The Book of Enoch, the Book of Jubilees, the
Assumption of Moses, the Ascension of Isaiah* and so on.
[2] Mk. iv. 11, 12.

sudden catastrophe. But only He understood
that. The early Church seems to have ignored
all those parables of slow growth and to have
expected sudden immediate return. They misunderstood Him just as, until Pentecost, they
altogether misunderstood the secret of His
Ministry.

For what is that secret? In any dramatic
story one finds the significance by looking for
the conflict. The first task for any critic
of tragedy is to find what are the opposing
parties in the tragic conflict. What are here
the opposing forces? Christ on the one side;
what on the other? Of course, we are
at first inclined to say, Sin; and that is right,
if we mean enough by the word "sin." But
it does not mean that the Lord's enemies were
of the criminal classes. The background of
darkness against which the Light of the
World stands out in its splendour is not sin
as we ordinarily conceive it; it is dead
religion. The great opposing force against
which Christ, in the days of His flesh, could
effect little was the established and self-
satisfied religion of the time; and once at
least He expressed His judgment that the

deadness of that religion was something
beyond the reach of the divine forgiveness.
What was it that had happened ? He had
healed a man possessed of a devil, and
those who watched asserted that He did this
in the power of the devil. He replies, That
is to suppose that the devil divides his house
against itself, which seems improbable : but it
is also to say of a plainly good thing that it is a
bad thing. And he adds, Say what you like
about Me ; " Whoso speaketh a word against
the Son of Man, it shall be forgiven him ; "
but if when the very spirit of goodness is at
work before you, you call it evil because it
happens not to fit into your scheme, then
there really is no hope ; " Whosoever speaketh
against the Holy Spirit, it shall not be
forgiven him, neither in this world, neither in
the world to come." [1] They were not
peculiarly wicked people ; they were the
upholders of a conventional righteousness :
but they were contented. That is always in
the Gospels the one hopeless condition. The
Pharisee praying in the temple was no doubt
a very much better man than the publican.

[1] Mt. xii. 22-32.

That is, in fact, the point of the parable ; he really was a good man according to the standards of the time ; but he was contented ; he was going to stay where he was and never get any better. He was content with thanking God that he was not as other men are. And the other man, who no doubt stood much lower in the moral scale at the moment, but knew his imperfections and his need of forgiveness and of growth, is justified rather than the Pharisee.[1]

So it is too in perhaps the most extra-ordinary of all the stories of the Gospels, when there was brought to the Lord a woman taken in adultery that He might pronounce judgment ; having first shamed into silence the accusers, He says to the woman, " Neither do I condemn thee ; go and sin no more."[2] It is possible to say, " Neither do I condemn thee ;" because it is also possible to say, with effect, " Go and sin no more." The one thing demanded is always the power to grow. Growth and progress in the spiritual life is the one thing Christ is always demanding ; and however low the moral state of any individual may be, provided that capacity for growth is

[1] Lk. xviii. 9-14,   [2] John viii. 1-11.

not lost, there is always hope, hope even of ultimate perfection. But however high the moral state may be, if perfection is not yet reached and the power of growth is gone, then the imperfection is permanent and salvation is impossible.

But it is not enough to learn that our Lord's one demand is for the power to grow and that the one deadly foe we have to meet is spiritual stagnation. What is it in which He requires that people shall grow? There is one ceremony and one ceremony only which He has commanded His disciples perpetually to celebrate. Let us go back behind all the theology, and all the meanings which have quite rightly gathered round that ceremony, to its first institution; let us think what it must have looked like to the people who were there, before they began to meditate upon it, and before they could find what it could do for them in their own lives. In a time of quite intense emotional stress—the last time that the Lord was to sup with His friends— He took bread and said that it was His body; and He gave thanks for it, He broke it, and He gave it to them and said,—" Do this in

H

not lost, there is always hoe, hope er
ultimate perfection. But hwever big
moral state may be, if perfetion is n
reached and the power of rowth is
then the imperfection is permanen
salvation is impossible.

But it is not enough to lear that our
one demand is for the power) grow a'
the one deadly foe we hre to
spiritual stagnation. What it in
requires that people shall row?
one ceremony and one cereony
He has commanded His disc
o celebrate. Let us go bac
heology, and all the meani
quite rightly gathered ror
o its first institution; '
must have looked like '
here, before they beg
nd   they co
o for them in their
uite intense emo'
hat the Lord w

remembrance of me." [1] He took the bread of
which He said it was His Body,—" This is My
Body : as I treat this bread, so I treat My
Body "—and He gave it to them ; and said,
" Do that if you want to show you remember
Me." Do what ? The sign, no doubt. But,
far more important, what it signifies. The
demand is nothing less than this, that men
should take their whole human life, and break it,
and give it for the good of others. The quality
in which we are to grow is service to the point
of absolute devotion and complete sacrifice.

Love, and the capacity to grow in love,
is the whole secret. And He in His own
life realises His own ideal. If one takes
all these precepts and sets over against them
the life itself from its relatively happy open-
ing, when the people flock to Him in Galilee,
to the dark conclusion in the Garden, before
Pilate, and on the Cross, all through we feel
that this quality of absolute selflessness is
manifest in perfect completeness. It would
never occur to anyone to say of Christ before
Pilate that He was a great man ; it would
never occur to anyone to say that He was

[1] Cor. xi. 23–25.

noble-minded ; all these expressions, which have about them some suggestion of dominance and the imposition of a man's own will upon others, are inappropriate. He rises superior to all about Him, not because He imposes His will upon them, but because He does not impose His will at all, because He has apparently no will of His own except to do what His Mission requires.

And so, both in His teaching and in His life, He is the climax of human ethics. For there is no morality beyond absolute devotion to the public good. That is the climax of morality ; you cannot go further. He taught it and He practised it. And He is the perfection also of human religion, for not only does He combine together all the strands that can be woven together in the religious life, but also His will is in perfect dependence upon the will of God. In His experience prayer was always answered; and it is His promise that whatsoever we ask in His name, in His spirit, will be answered, for it will be the will of God. There is the fact ; there at least are just a few, a very few, of the leading features of that great fact.

How are we to understand it? We will
not attempt to-day either to grasp more fully
than before a theological system or (still less)
to formulate a new one. Let us rather go
back to a document which we were careful
last time not to consider, the Fourth Gospel.
Now there is a great dispute about the
question who wrote the Fourth Gospel.
I cannot help thinking that it does not very
much matter. The writer had either been
present at the scenes which he records, as I
believe, or else He was absolutely steeped in
the record of that Life. In either case He is
finding in that story the manifestation of the
divine Christ with whom he is in daily
communion. It is perfectly clear, for
instance, that the style of the discourses
belongs to the writer and not to our Lord. If
the Lord spoke as He speaks in the Synoptic
Gospels, then He did not speak as He speaks
in the Gospel of St. John. It is quite clear
also, as the writer says himself, that he
selects episodes specially adapted to bring out
the lessons which He wishes to teach.[1]   Here
then we have a writer who is not merely

[1] John xx. 30–31.

recording what he remembers, or has heard, of the Lord's life, but is exhibiting the identity between the historic Christ and the spiritual Christ of religious communion. And thus the Gospel fulfils what would otherwise be a great need in the New Testament. In the Synoptists we have the outward facts recorded; in St. Paul's Epistles we have the theory of those facts gradually evolved by one who perhaps had never seen the Lord, who stood at a little distance, who looked at the great Fact and tried to estimate its value and meaning. But so the Lord had become rather remote. The risen, glorified Christ of St. Paul's Epistles, if taken alone and apart from the Gospel narrative, would not have the intimacy of human appeal which we need. In St. John we have one who writes with the whole wealth of Pauline meditation at his disposal, and who then reveals the absolute identity of that human Figure in Palestine with the divine Spirit known in the communion of the worshipper.

And this makes the Gospel surely not less valuable, but more so. It is the inspired comment on the old story, the comment of one who can fitly be represented as saying,

> "To me that story, ay, that life and death
> Of which I wrote, It was, to me, it is,
> Is here and now ; I apprehend nought else."[1]

How does he set about the great task ? He begins with a conception almost universally accepted at the time, just as it is almost universally accepted now, although its name is now generally different,—the conception of the divine Word or Logos. Everyone at any rate understood what was meant by the prologue of St. John's Gospel ; it was common property. The theory had been elaborated by the Stoics and had been combined with Jewish speculation by Philo. Everyone would understand it : and it would serve not only to bring the Gospel into relation with the modes of thought habitual to the people for whom it is written, but it would also serve to bring out the full significance of that life, or at any rate more of the significance than previous attempts had been able to do. It was of no use to say to a Gentile

---

[1] Browning, *A Death in the Desert.* (The best commentary on St. John's Gospel)

community that the Messiah was come ; they had not been brought up to expect any Messiah to come ; it would be an announcement wholly without interest for them. But to say that the indwelling principle of the world, which governs everything, has been made manifest in a single Life is to say something whose importance is beyond all parallel. They believed, as we believe, that the world is a single system governed by a single principle ; and there is nothing which matters so much as to know the character of that principle. St. John says that this principle, the Logos, by whom all things were made, and without whom was not anything made which was made, became flesh in Christ. We are to see there the character of the principle or spirit which made the world and holds it in being, —nothing less than that ; and he constructs his narrative in such a way as to bring out this character.

The Gospel falls of itself into five sections. It is a kind of spiritual drama in five acts. The first section consists of the first four chapters. There is the Prologue ; and then there is the introduction of Christ to four different types of persons. First to the fore-runner, the predecessor, who recognises and yields before his greater Follower. Secondly to the group of disciples who follow because of what another, namely John the Baptist, tells them; and then to another group of disciples who follow because the Lord calls them Himself; as that exhausts the ways in which men can come to the Lord there is no need to give the call of any other disciples. Then we have the introduction to Nicodemus, the religious leader who wished to come by night and in secret, spying out the new movement, and is very directly told that unless he is moved by the inscrutable influence of the Spirit to join it openly he can never enter into its triumph: "Except a man be born again he cannot see the Kingdom of God." Lastly there is the simple woman of Samaria, to whom the truth is quite plainly told, and by whom it is accepted. There you have typical introductions.

All this is followed by a long controversy between the Lord and the Jews, represented in this Gospel in sharp antagonism as the forces of light and darkness. This section occupies chapters V to XII. Very steadily the gulf widens; the controversy becomes more and more acute, until at the last moment, when the breach is complete, seeing no doubt a strange significance in the fact, St. John reports the advent of those first Greeks who came to see the Lord, the first fruits of the Gentile world: and the section culminates with a very definite proclamation of the central principle of the Gospel; "Except a corn of wheat fall into the ground, and die, it abideth alone; but if it die it bringeth forth much fruit. And I, if I be lifted up from the earth, will draw all men unto Me." [1]

The next section, the section most familiar to Christian readers, occupies chapters XIII to XVII; here the Lord is alone with His friends, and prepares them for the crisis that is to follow. Then there are two very short sections; first chapters XVIII and XIX, which tell of the apparent triumph of the forces of darkness, and then chapter XX, which records the actual triumph of the Lord. Chapter XXI is, no doubt, an epilogue.

Scattered through this story the evangelist

[1] John xii. 24, 32.

records seven miracles representing seven great stages of the spiritual life.[1] (1) There is the changing water into wine : the change which Christ will bring about in our spiritual condition is as the change from water to wine. (2) The healing of the nobleman's son : the absolute necessity of faith, without which we cannot receive blessing. (3) The healing of the impotent man : the restoration of the powers which we lost in the wasted years before our contact with the Lord. (4) The feeding of the five thousand : Christ the sustenance of all our life. (5) The walking on the water, with the incident, mentioned only by St. John, that the moment He reached the boat they were at the land : Christ the unseen Guide in all our troubles. (6) The healing of the man born blind : Christ the source of light, so that we no longer need external guidance. (7) The raising of Lazarus : Christ the source of all our life. And this interpretation of the miracles is not fanciful, because to many of the miracles there is appended a long discourse bringing out their spiritual meaning.

[1] John, ii. 1-11; iv 46-54; v. 1-9; vi. 1-14; vi. 16-21; ix. 1-7; xi. 1-46.

There are some quite definite points that emerge in the Gospel to which I would like to call attention. It is pre-eminently the Gospel of Divine Immanence. It begins with the conception of the immanence in the world of a principle, the Logos, or Word; it is the manifestation of the indwelling God. But all through the Incarnate Word refers to "Him that sent Me" as some one above and beyond Himself. And that is a step that we must take. We found in the first lecture that we cannot in the last resort understand the world at all, except by regarding it as the expression of a purpose, which must be rooted in a Will. To speak about an immanent purpose is very good sense; but to speak about a purpose behind which there is no Will is nonsense; and to speak about an immanent will is nonsense. It is the purpose, the meaning and thought of God, that is immanent, not God Himself. He is not limited to the world that He has made; He is beyond it, the source and ground of it all, but not it. Just as you may say that in Shakespeare's work his thoughts and feelings are immanent; you find them there in the

book ; but you don't find Shakespeare, the
living, thinking, acting man, in the book.
You have to infer the kind of being that he
was from what he wrote ; he himself is not
there ; his thoughts are there. And so we
must follow St. John very carefully ; for, in
our interest in insisting upon the divine
immanence, we are in danger of forgetting
that God is a Spirit who makes the world,
upon whose will it depends, but who is not
the sum total of its natural laws.

One might say a good deal about the
treatment in this Gospel of the problem of
evil ; but as that problem is to occupy us next
time I shall pass it by. But something must
be said about the relation here shown between
Christ and the Spirit. St John keeps the
two sides of this question both fully before
us. Only through Christ can the Spirit come ;
" There was not yet Spirit, because that Jesus
was not yet glorified " ; [1] only through Him,
only through His historic Life, can the Spirit
come. But also the work of that historic
Life is not complete for us so long as it
remains a mere historic event. The Spirit

---

[1] John vii. 39 (see Greek and discussion of reading).

that was in Christ must become through Him
the Spirit in us. "It is expedient for you
that I go away : for if I go not away, the
Comforter will not come unto you ; but if I
depart I will send Him unto you."[1] The
historic fact is the only means by which the
Spirit can be brought ; it exists in order to
bring the Spirit and must never be isolated
from the gift of the Spirit which follows.
So we find all the post-Resurrection appearances of this Gospel emphasize the need of
turning from the historic to the spiritual.
There is the appearance to Mary at the tomb.
"Cling not to Me" (as it should be trans-
lated), "for I am not yet ascended"; it is not
to the historic finite Christ that we are to
cling, but to the glorified Christ of spiritual
experience. There is the appearance to the
ten in the Upper Chamber when " He breathed
on them and saith unto them, Receive ye the
Holy Spirit"; the Spirit of His life is to be,
as it were, the breath of their lives. And
then there is the appearance to Thomas,
supplying him with the external evidence
that he needed, but leading to the words,

John xvi. 7.

" Blessed are they that have not seen, and yet have believed." This spirit has to become the spirit of our life ; and only so far as it does so, according to this Gospel, is the work of Christ complete.[1]

What then is this Spirit ? We have arrived at the point to which our consideration of the fact of Christ led us, that He is the manifestation of absolute human morality and religion ; and because He is that, St. John tells us He is the expression in human language of absolute Godhead : His character reveals the character of God. " He that hath seen Me hath seen the Father."[2] So then, we shall learn from Him what is the real type of human life for us to follow ; and what is the divine life into which we are to enter through His life. The divine life is the Christ life ; Heaven is the Cross. That, I would almost say, is the central thought of the whole of this Gospel. " We beheld His glory " ;[3] all through what is being revealed is the glory of the Son of God. But the emphasis on the term " glory " becomes more

[1] John xx. 11-18 ; 19-23 ; 26-29. Chapter xxi. is not part of the original scheme of the Gospel.
[2] John xiv. 9.   [3] John i. 14.

and more complete as the Passion approaches ; and becomes greatest just at the moment when our Lord is dedicating Himself to the last Sacrifice. He opens the prayer of self-consecration to that sacrifice with the words, " Father, the hour is come ; glorify Thy Son, that Thy Son also may glorify Thee. . . . I have glorified Thee on the earth ; I have finished the work which Thou gavest me to do. And now, O Father, glorify Thou Me with Thine own self with the glory which I had with Thee before the world was." [1] The eternal glory is to be fully manifested when the self-surrender and the self-sacrifice is complete. The divine life, to which we are called through Christ, is not then a life of enjoyment purchased by temporary sacrifice ; it is the sacrifice ; and there is no reward beyond except the triumph of the cause for which the man is sacrificed. There is no appeal to human selfishness in the Christian doctrine of the divine reward for virtue ; for the reward is simply the demand for further sacrifice. There may come a time when absolute self-surrender brings no pain, but

[1] John xvii. 1. 4, 5 : cf. xii. 23, 24.

only the intensest joy, such as love brings
when it is returned ; meanwhile the surrender
and the sacrifice itself is realised as the
greatest treasure in the world. The Divine
Life is the Christ Life ; Heaven is the Cross.

The further implications of this must be
left for another lecture ; but in connection
with it we go back to the historic Christ and
understand Him perhaps more fully. We
like, it may be, to think of Him as saying,
" Come unto Me all ye that labour and are
heavy laden and I will give you rest." [1] Yes
if we *are* heavy laden, if we *have* taken upon
ourselves the burden of the world's misery
and sin, then the promise is for us that the
yoke shall be easy and the burden light.
But if not, then there is another saying of
Christ recorded in the Synoptic Gospels,
which perhaps has more applicability. St.
Peter had confessed that He was the Messiah ;
and one of the things which was expected of the
Messiah was that he should lead a triumphal
procession into Jerusalem, that He might take
possession of the throne of His father David.
And He says, There will be a Messianic

[1] Mt. xi. 28.

ꞮCession, but it will not be the kind of
g you expect. What it will look like
ꞮROcession of condemned criminals. " If
Ɪ an will come after Me, let him ignore
Ɪ ꞮꞮself and take up his cross and follow Me." [1]
Wholesale crucifixions were not so very
uncommon at that time; the picture would
have been vivid enough, each man carrying
his own gallows to the place of execution.

That is the demand. The fact and the
interpretation tally. If Christ was what St.
John tells us, the manifestation of the divine
Word, then He has the right to make that
claim upon us; not otherwise. And if it has
been found, as it has been found over and
over again, that in experience the people
who answer the demand receive the promise,
then the historic Christ must be the Christ of
St. John's theology.

Mk. viii. 34.

LECTURE V

WE have considered the Personality who is in every sense the pivot of the Christian faith and the Christian philosophy; but we have to go further in order to understand that Personality, if we may, at least in some degree, not only in Himself but in His relation to the whole of our experience. The field is obviously far too wide to be covered in one lecture, but it is nothing short of this which the doctrine of the Atonement really undertakes. And the doctrine of the Atonement is absolutely central, in the sense that what we all of us need of our religion is primarily that it should throw some light upon the mystery of Evil.

When we say that we hope in some degree to understand what it is that the historic life of Christ stands for, not only in our own experience but in the history of the world, we mean that we hope to see it in relation to all other facts.   That is all one can ever mean by understanding ; but such understanding is, I think, peculiarly necessary at the present moment, because there is a tendency in some places to suggest that we can do very well without understanding our religion at all, seeing that it is a great spiritual experience which comes upon men, which is its own evidence, and which is only spoilt by any attempt to make it intelligible.   It must be taken, we are told, as the breaking in upon the world of some Power not otherwise to be discovered in the world, a Power from which we hope for our own and for the world's Redemption ; but if it is thus alien from the normal process of the world, it is impossible, on the face of it, to relate it to the other facts of the world ; it must be taken apart from them altogether as something unique and it is almost a profanity to suggest that it can be intelligible at all.

Now the motive which prompts such a contention we must all respect, for it is the motive of reverence, and of fear lest in our clumsy hands the beauty of the truth should suffer. And yet when we come to the problem of Evil, the most real of all problems, no one is content with dreams; everyone insists that what is believed must be established. It is not enough to say, " I have felt it; and I am sure that what I have felt is true." The man who is really at grips with evil, whether in his own life or in the world, will require some further assurance than another individual's ecstatic feelings. We must have an intelligible scheme of salvation; we must have it, because precisely those people who most need the saving force are unable to receive it unless it is in some degree intelligible. There is this permanent paradox about evil, that it is itself the chief obstacle, intellectually, to a belief in God, and yet it constitutes the chief motive for desiring God. We may have noticed how differently people were affected by the earthquake at Messina. Some people (mostly, I am inclined to suspect, reading about it in their arm-chairs, and writing about it in well-appointed studies) urged in the *Spectator* and other eminently respectable journals, that this catastrophe made it very difficult to believe in God. But you will find other people who say that, in face of such a fact, life is unbearable without God. And then one begins to realise that, though a religion may be a poor thing, which only comes into operation in so far as we are depressed or overcome by the evil of the world, yet it is true that the evil in the world is the main force which drives us back upon God, if God there be. So we have this great paradox : the same fact which seems at first sight irresistible evidence against the existence of God, is itself the chief cause of our demand for the existence of God.

Let us, then, try to consider in the first place a perfectly general form of the problem. As far as the argument is concerned the earthquake at Messina is no more difficult than an ordinary headache. Why is there any evil in the world at all ? That is the problem ; and we have already seen in our first lecture that Why? means, For what purpose ? The problem of evil is always a problem in terms of purpose. No one is much interested in finding out how it came

here, as a matter of historical fact; that does
not much matter.   The problem is, what is it
doing here? What is it for? Why does God
permit it?   Or, if God is omnipotent, in
which case permission and creation are the
same, why did God create it?   While we are
sitting at our ease it generally seems to us
that the world would be very much better if
all evil were abolished, and indeed had never
existed.   But would it?   Which are our own
best days,—the days when we have nothing
to perplex us, or trouble us? or the days
when, at considerable cost to ourselves, we
have made some real effort against the evil
which afflicted either ourselves or other people?
Surely the latter.   Surely we know that one
of the best of the good things in life is victory
and particularly moral victory.   But to demand victory without an antagonist is to
demand something with no meaning.   If, then,
goodness is to exist up to the limit of what
even we can understand, there must at least
be an antagonist to be overcome.   If you take
all the evil out of the world you will remove
the possibility of the best thing in life.   That
does not mean that evil is good.   What one

means by calling a thing good is that the spirit rests permanently content with it for its own sake. Evil is precisely that with which no spirit can rest content ; and yet it is the condition, not the accidental but the essential condition, of what is in and for itself the best thing in life, namely moral victory.

That, of course, is a perfectly general treatment of the subject, which does not for a moment touch any particular case ; it only tells us in general terms that evil at least may be conducive to a total excellence of the world greater than is possible or conceivable without the existence of evil. It also tells us that the actual solution of the problem of evil in any particular case is to be found by destroying that evil and wringing out of it the victory of which it is the possible condition : so that in the end our solution of the actual evil in the world is not to be found by sitting down and thinking, but by searching out all the evil we can find and fighting it ; only when it is beaten, does it become an element in the total good of the world. And this is true even of evils that are past : for it is not the case, when you are speaking of values, that the past is unalterable. The facts of the past may be unalterable ; its meaning and value is not. If its meaning were unalterable, atonement would be impossible. But just consider two plays, each in three acts, one passing from gloom through a neutral state to joy, and the other reversing the process ; it is not the case that the total emotional value of those two plays is identical because the average emotional value of the three acts is identical. On the contrary, the former is supremely exhilarating (more so than a play which is joyous throughout), and the latter supremely depressing (more so than a play which is gloomy throughout). So it may be in the history of the world. If there is any ground discoverable for saying that the history of the world is really a continuous and progressive moral victory, then it will appear true that all the evil, bad as it is, and precisely because it is so bad, is an element in the total goodness of the whole · we shall only realise that goodness in so far as we side with the forces that are triumphing over the evil, in so far as we assist in the victory. But if victory is good, and if victorious spiritual excellence is something better than an untroubled innocence, then, granted that the evil is overcome, it is better that it should first exist.

And now let us apply this in some detail, if we may. First of all we must notice that there are three main forms of evil—intellectual evil which we call Error, emotional evil which we call Pain, and moral evil which we call Sin. The problem of Error I must ask you to excuse me from treating, because it would take us very far away from the main theme of these lectures. Obviously, if what we say is true, it must be applicable to the problem of Error ; but the application is not possible here and now.

For Pain there have been three types of consolation, and, so far as I know, three only. There is the Stoic type (still, I suppose, though I speak in great ignorance, the dominant attitude of the Mahomedan world), which bids us rise superior to it : "It is the will of God ; to the wise these things are nugatory." But that does not help us, if we are not wise ; and I think it is the case that nearly all the great Stoics were people in comfortable circumstances. There is also the

Epicurean answer, which is in essence much the same as the answer of most of the great religions of the East : " It is but for a time ; soon we fall asleep in the unending slumber." That is consolation of a sort. And there is one other answer : " Christ also suffered" ; and that, I venture to suggest, with the Christian interpretation of Christ, is a real and even adequate solution. If it is true that Christ is the manifestation of the divine Life, then it is also true that in our sufferings we are entering into the secret of the divine life, provided we bear them in His Spirit. And does not that as a matter of fact satisfy us ?

There are two ways, in which, it seems to me, pain or suffering is justified as an element in a world for which we claim that it represents the purpose of an omnipotent and all-loving God : in the first place it is surely true that, so far as suffering meets with real sympathy (and if God is the father of Jesus Christ, all suffering finds real sympathy in Him), it has become a positive gain both to the sufferer and to the sympathiser. It is not easy to argue such a question ; people think so or they do not. One cannot ever argue about questions of value; but I will only ask that we should try to think of these subjects with our imaginations alive.   For, of course, the moment our imaginations are slack, the moment we begin to talk prose, we lose sight altogether of the real fact and only think how disagreeable pain is.   Of course, it is disagreeable; that is why we call it pain.   But are we going to say that all things that are disagreeable are bad ?   I do not think that would have been the attitude, or is the attitude, of any martyr who is a real martyr. They "rejoiced that they were counted worthy to suffer." [1]   St. Paul rejoiced that he was able " to fill up that which is behind of the afflictions of Christ." [2]   There is no suggestion that it would be better if the suffering could be avoided.   Suffering must not be sought for its own sake, for it is an evil ; but if it comes in the course of a life's devotion to some great cause, the true devotee will welcome it.   This is the second justification of Pain, its value when gladly endured for a worthy cause.

But I must hurry on to the crucial point.

[1] Acts v. 41.   [2] Col. i. 24.

How can sin be part of a perfect whole planned by Almighty God? And how can sin itself ever be overcome and done away? Is it not a vital flaw in the world?

Now, of course, if you take the world as it is at the present moment and stop there, and do not consider at all what is to come out of it, then the evil in it is a vital flaw; the world as it exists is very largely bad; and if its present condition is all that can ever be, then the problem of evil is insoluble. But then too either God is not omnipotent or He is not good. But what do we mean by sin? Always, surely, in the last resort, self-will. All the actions which under certain circumstances are sinful may under other circumstances be right: the impulses which prompt them have their place in the whole economy of human nature. Sin is the self-assertion, either of a part of a man's nature against the whole, or of a single member of the human family against the welfare of that family and the will of its Father. But if it is self-will, how can it be overcome? Not by any kind of force; for force cannot bend the will. Not by any kind of external transaction; that may remit the penalty, but will not of itself change the will. It must be by the revelation of a love so intense that no heart which beats can remain indifferent to it. Then the self-will may be overcome. To that part of the question we will return. But if that were true, would it not also be true that we should find some value even for this? Yes, surely; for the struggle and the sacrifice, which love goes through in that self-manifestation, enter into the fibre of the love itself. Love consists in the giving away of self for others. Whatever makes that giving away of self more complete, whatever makes it absolute and final, is a help to the perfecting of love. Would you rather have a world that had never sinned, or a world that has sinned and been redeemed through the sacrifice of Christ? To my mind, only one answer is possible. A redeemed world is infinitely greater in moral worth; its moral achievement taken as a whole, its spiritual value, is something out of all proportion to that of a world which has simply never known what wrong is. And this harmonises with what we found before, that the one thing on which our Lord insists

is always the power to grow in love ; and we
remember the parables which close with
the saying that "joy shall be in heaven
over one sinner that repenteth more than
over ninety and nine just persons, that need
no repentance." [1]   The growth in love, and
the sacrifice which evokes that growth in love,
are, I would suggest, the most precious thing
in life.   Take away the conditions of this and
you will destroy the value of the spiritual
world.   In St. John's Gospel the manifestation of the Divine Glory is completed in
the Death of Christ upon the Cross; it is
only in the death-struggle with evil that the
full splendour of absolute goodness is realised.
Moreover, evil, having occasioned the sacrifice,
is itself conquered by it ; it is condemned by
the condemnation it pronounces on the Lord,
and won over by the Death which it inflicts.
"Now is the judgment of this world ; now
shall the prince of this world be cast out.
And I, if I be lifted up from the earth, will
draw all men unto me." [2]   Considering how
rigid this writer is in his distinction between
children of light and children of darkness, we

---

[1] Lk. xv. 3–10 : cf. 11–32 and v. 32.   [2] Jn. xii. 31, 32

cannot doubt that, when he said " all men," he meant it.   Thus, when the breach between good and evil is complete and the sacrifice it leads to is imminent, we find that this very sacrifice is to heal the breach.

But now let us try to consider, if we may, how this is actually effected, as the Church claims, by the Life and Death of Christ ; and I am afraid I must ask you to pardon me while I mention some of the older theories on the subject, because it is necessary that we should gather together all the main elements which have entered into the experience of the Church.

The first theory which attained to very great importance, after the Apostolic age, is that of the Greek theologians, to whom everything turns upon the union of the divine and human substance.   The Greeks had very little conception, if any, of spiritual individuality : they had very little apprehension of the fact that, because I am I, I am not anybody else.   They thought of great human qualities which subsisted unchanged in different people. The humanity of all of us, they thought, is the same : and if humanity has been taken

into the Godhead, then, in that action, all
persons who have humanity were redeemed.
They also had practically no psychology of
the will, and they were, therefore, unable
to state the problem in strictly moral terms.
For them redemption was a change of substance, not a transformation of the will. And
also they had no general doctrine of progress,
such as has been introduced into our thought
mainly through biological evolution; and
consequently they were unable to regard the
world as steadily progressing from lower to
higher, and had to regard salvation as a
complete change from one fixed state to
another fixed state.

The chief theologian of that period is, no
doubt, St. Athanasius; and it is important that
we should understand the significance of his
controversy with the Arians. It arose entirely
from the necessity, under which the Greeks
lay, of thinking in terms of substance. The
starting of both was the Logos-doctrine. The
Logos-doctrine, in pre-Christian thought, had
been the means of explaining how the world
came to be made by the infinite unchanging
God; the Logos, the divine Word, was inter-

polated between the supreme God and the world as Mediator of Creation. But if He was to mediate between the divine substance and the perishable substance of this world, He must not Himself be of one substance with the Father, for then He would not be a Mediator at all. On the other side, if human substance is to be redeemed by the infusion of the divine into human nature, then it is essential that the Redeemer should be of one substance with the Father; and the whole controversy really turned on the question whether Christianity was to be a particular form of Neo-Platonic philosophy or a religion of redemption. That was the question at issue. To us the difference between "one substance" and "like substance" has very little meaning because we do not habitually think in terms of "substance" at all. To them it meant simply everything. The Arians were concentrating attention upon the problem of Creation, which is secondary; for here the world is, however it got here. Athanasius was concentrating attention on the doctrine of Redemption; and that is primary.

Now the Greek method of thinking alwayꜱ

involves the difficulty that it puts the moral problem rather in the background. But there was one thing it seized upon with quite unequalled force, and that was the experience of the Christian's unity with his Master. "He became Man," as St. Athanasius said, "in order that we might be made divine." [1] In Christ was accomplished the union of the human and divine Natures, which is at once the Incarnation and the Atonement; it is in that union of Natures that everything is found; and the basis of that conception, which made it so important to those thinkers, is the experience that Christ was with them, that they were mystically one with Christ, in the way which St. Paul expresses "To me to live is Christ"; "I live; yet not I, but Christ liveth in me." [2]

The next great stage which we must consider for a moment is that of St. Augustine and his controversy with the Pelagians: and here we arrive, as I think, at the real root of the problem. Pelagius' position, put shortly, was, —"I can be good if I will. God rewards me when I am good; but does not make me good.

[1] *De Incarnatione*, 54.　　[2] Phil. i. 21; Gal. ii. 20.

His reward is, of course, an incentive to goodness but it is no more ; and God's connection
with the moral struggle is confined to the
promise of reward or the threat of punishment."
Augustine in effect replies,—"I could be good,
if I would ; but I won't." And 'that is the
whole difficulty : I cannot move my will. My
will moves everything else ; but what is to
move it, if it is diseased and is set on the
things which I know are wrong? What in
the world will cure that? The whole
difficulty is, that when the opportunity of
wrong-doing comes, I always choose it ; how
am I to cure myself? And I do not think
there is any writer who has ever grasped this
absolute impotence of the human will with
greater vigour than Augustine ; and his
answer is, that the revelation of God in
Christ supplies a new force, which he calls
Grace, which comes upon us from without and
changes us. His whole insistence is that we,
by ourselves, cannot work out our own
salvation, or even our own claim to salvation.
We are quite helpless ; sin consists in the
disease of the will ; and if the will is diseased
it cannot cure itself. If a man is in the state

of Augustine himself when he prayed, " Give me chastity, but not yet!" he is, if left to himself, incurable.

Now we notice that in the Greek theory, whatever its form, and in the Augustinian theory, nothing appears to be said about the Death of Christ. The Greeks, of course, dealt with the Death of Christ, almost always regarding it as a ransom paid to the devil, by which God bought us back from the just dominion of the devil, under which the Fall had brought us. That theory of the Death of Christ held the field on the whole, so far as I know, until St. Anselm, and it was still defended with passion by St. Bernard in his controversy with Abelard. St. Anselm is really the author, more than anyone else, of the doctrine of the Atonement which has prevailed in Western Christendom from that time onwards. His position in effect is this. We owe a debt to God, because His claim upon us is for absolute obedience ; and even if we obey for the whole of the future, there is still the past unredeemed. And the magnitude of our debt is to be measured by the Majesty against which we have offended. We have

incurred, therefore, an infinite debt which, because it is infinite, we cannot pay ; only God
can pay it.   But it must be paid by Man, for it
is Man who has sinned.   God, therefore, must
become man ; the God-Man being sinless need
not die, for death is the punishment of sin.
His death, therefore, will be something over
and above what is required of Him, and will
constitute merit and a claim upon God which
He can plead for those who by His Incarnation
are His fellow-men, provided they will present
themselves before the Father in His Name.
That is to say, the position is very nearly the
position commonly known as "vicarious
satisfaction." [1]   The difficulties about it are
these : first, that it sets out from a conception
of God as offended and needing to be appeased ;
and secondly, that it concentrates attention
upon delivery from the punishment of sin,
and not upon delivery from the sin itself.
Consequently it has a tendency to a certain
self-centredness which is not wholly Christian.
But it has this great gain, that it speaks,

---

[1] It is important to distinguish this from "Vicarious suffering,"
a principle everywhere operative (for all over the world good
people suffer through the fault of bad people), and most con-
spicuously in the case of Christ.

as Augustine had spoken, in moral terms, and treats the problem as a problem of guilt, and expresses the central truth that God takes upon Himself the burden of the sin of the world.

At about the same time at which that theory arose, there arose also the simple theory of Abelard, that Christ by His manifestation of His love awakens love in us, and that this is the Atonement. This was denounced by St. Bernard, apparently because St. Bernard could only think in legal terms and required that there should be a definite transaction. And yet what Abelard said is a thing which every Christian is prepared to say, though he may wish to add more.

Now let us see if it is not possible, with the help of modern thought, to construct for ourselves a doctrine which, of course, will not be exhaustive of all the mystery of the Atonement, but which may, none the less, set before us that mystery under a form which makes it no longer baffling to the intelligence, but rather something which we can receive as rational, something which we have begun to understand and which we hope in time to understand more fully.

We go back to St. John who has the key
to all our modern problems : we begin by
asking what is the character of God, what is
His relation to us, and particularly what is
His relation to us when we sin ? We see it
in Christ. " He that hath seen Me hath seen
the Father." [1] In Christ's Agony we see what
our sin costs God ; and in His bearing before
His enemies we see how God regards us as we
inflict the blow; " when He was reviled He
reviled not again, when He suffered He
threatened not." [2] We cannot go on wounding One who accepts our wounds like that ;
we are filled with fear, not the old craven
fear of punishment, but the fear of wounding
the tenderest of all hearts. " There is mercy
with Thee, *therefore* shalt Thou be feared." [3]
And in this, which sounds so simple, I believe
there is contained every valuable element
that was present in any of the great historic
theories of the Atonement. We realise our
own absolute impotence to change ourselves;
but we realise also that we are changed as we
contemplate the love of God revealed in
Christ ; we realise that we owe to God some-

<hr>

[1] Jn. xiv. 9.   [2] I Pet. ii. 23.   [3] Ps. cxxx. 4.

thing that we can never pay, but which in
His love He remits as though it were paid
already; and we realise an absolute unity
between ourselves and Him as something
which is at least possible, and is beginning
already to be actual, because to love like that
we must respond with love; and love is the
union of spirits. All the great elements
come in. The great difficulty about the
theory of Abelard was that it never showed
us *how* the death of Christ was the revelation
of His love; the suffering of One so gentle
and so perfect must awaken sympathy; but
we need to see how the suffering itself flows
from the love. That we find, if we take
St. John's great guiding principle, that in
Christ we see the Father, so that in His
attitude to His enemies we see God's attitude
to us when we are at enmity with Him (for
He is never at enmity with us),—" Father,
forgive them; for they know not what they
do." [1] I believe that if we work out that
theory, thinking of the effect which love
always has, when it is understood, upon any
heart, and remembering that the world has

[1] Lk. xxiii. 34.

progressed a good deal since the earliest ages that we know, and progressed in love more perhaps than in any other quality, we shall find that it may be true that the whole world is moving onwards for ever under the impulse of the infinite love of God to a more and more adequate return of that love; we begin to think of the whole Universe as knit together in that love as its one controlling principle. Love works by sacrifice; that is always the mode of love's operation. But that sacrifice is not the means of appeasing anger; it is the outcome of love and of love alone. We shall never be true either to our own best thought, or to the religious experience that is enshrined in the New Testament, unless we are resolute in setting out always from the love of God. "God commendeth His love toward us, in that, while we were yet sinners, Christ died for us." "God so loved the world that He gave His only begotten Son." [1]

It may be objected that this view of the Atonement is purely "subjective," and that the Christian experience demands something

---

[1] Rom. v. 8; Jn. iii. 16.

more " objective."   But what exactly is meant
by this ?   Is it meant that the Atonement is
accomplished altogether *outside* us, or that it
is something done *for* us, which we could
never do for ourselves ? These two are
compatible, but they are not identical.   The
view I have outlined insists that we could
never accomplish our own Atonement ; it is
done *for* us, and we have only to accept what
is so done.   But our theory also insists that
though done *for* us, it is accomplished *in* us.
The Atonement was completed on Calvary
in the sense that the Love of God then first
became fully manifest and thus attained its
full power to redeem ; the Atoning power
then came fully into the world.   But the
Atonement in the sense of full salvation, is
not complete until every soul knows the Love
of God and responds to it with answering
love.   Nor would it be true to say that we
are reducing it to a change of will for the
present and the future, the whole of the past
being ignored ; for we have seen that the
meaning and value of the past has still to
be determined by the events of the present
and future.   When the Love of God in Christ

has altogether conquered me, and changed me, my past sin will be the occasion of my loving Him, not only as King, but as Redeemer.

I know, of course, that it is possible to parody this view so as to make it a most pernicious lie, which tells a man not to trouble about sin for it is " only moral growing-pains." The danger of that lie, as of every lie that is dangerous, depends on the half-truth it perverts. Sin is the condition of what for me is the highest attainable state—the love of God in Christ my Redeemer. But it only becomes in fact the condition of that blessing in so far as I hate it with all my soul. Then, when I loathe it, it is the stepping-stone on which I rise ; but while I am content with it, it is evil and not good at all. Yet it only exists in me because (with part of my nature at least) I am content with it. I only do what is wrong because I like it. And therefore I cannot loathe it with my whole soul unless something lays hold on my affections and will, and changes them. " It is no more I that do it but sin which dwelleth in me. . . . . O wretched man that I am ! who shall deliver me out of the body of this death ?　I thank God through Jesus Christ our Lord." [1]

Or again, it may be said that we are leaving out of sight the justice of God; and again we must ask, what do we mean by the Divine Justice ?　In the sense of treating all men equally, God is certainly just; He is no respecter of persons.　But so far as justice means the infliction of pain on those who do wrong, without any intention to benefit them thereby, it is no virtue.　Retributive punishment is always either non-moral or immoral; a man has moral evil in him, and you add physical evil; what is the good of doing that ? Of course, if the pain or physical evil has the effect of curing the moral evil, its infliction is justifiable; but the notion that wickedness *ought* somehow to be balanced by pain seems to me wholly without foundation.

Are we to say then that God is not angry at sin, that He is incapable of moral indignation ?　Certainly not.　Love can be indignant.　A father can be indignant at the ingratitude of the son he loves.　But he does not wish his son evil; the anger and the

---

[1] Rom. vii. 20, 24, 25.

indignation, with the actions they prompt, are such as may be compatible with love.

If the Cross is the symbol of the pain our sin inflicts on God, it is thereby the symbol of the antagonism between sin and God. Between sin and His Nature there is utter enmity, and only through what we see in the Agony and Death is He victorious. That pain, we must suppose, is coloured and suffused with the knowledge of the victory beyond, but it is none the less real. The Epistle to the Hebrews maintains that " for the joy that was set before Him " Christ " endured ";[1] but does not suggest that the " endurance " was unreal.

And the Cross is the symbol also of what sin costs man. In Christ we see God, but only because we first see man. The desolation, the sense of desertion and hopeless failure and irremediable defeat : these are the elements that constitute the horror of great darkness which sin creates and through which we must pass to its destruction.

Gethsemane and Calvary are what sin costs to God and man. God's unchanging love

[1] Heb. xii. 2.

endures the mocking and the scourging and the thorns; Man's self-will must undergo them too, that it may learn its own destructiveness; yet the thorns make up the crown of the King of Love, and the Cross is the throne from which God holds sway over our hearts.

Keeping a steady hold on the Love of God as our one all-sufficing principle, and making a wise use of the conceptions of Personality and Evolution, which play so large a part in our modern thought, we shall be able to catch more of the meaning of the revelation of God in Christ than was possible, perhaps, in earlier times. The seat of the problem is our wills; they need transforming. It is not a change of " substance," but a love of things which now we do not love, that must be wrought in us. But though I am myself and no one else (so that the assumption of Humanity by God in Christ does not of itself unite me to God), yet I am social in every fibre of my being; to the appeal of love, if once I have heard and understood it, I cannot be indifferent; and Christ includes my personality in His own, and with His own presents it to the Father, because the appeal of His love is gradually conquering my heart, and consequently His purpose is gradually taking possession of my will. But the process is gradual, and there is no utter breach between the Human and the Divine; rather we should say that, because men are spiritual as God is spiritual, it is possible for God to reveal Himself in a human life; but because men are sinful, it takes all the ages for that self-revelation to win them to Himself. As the veil of self-love is drawn from the eyes of our soul, we appreciate Him more fully and are transformed more completely to His likeness. "We all, with unveiled face reflecting as a mirror the glory of the Lord, are transformed into the same image from glory to glory, even as from the Lord the Spirit." "We know that, if He shall be manifested, we shall be like Him; for we shall see Him as He is."[1]

Our Atonement then is accomplished through our realisation of the love of God. But how are we to believe that God is loving in this sense? If it is true that He made the whole world and all that is in it, and that we know Him only through the revelation of

_____
[1] II Cor. iii. 18 (R.V.); I John iii. 2 (R.V.)

Himself that He has given in Creation and in Inspiration, then how can we say that the Maker of this Universe is a God of infinite love? And I think we cannot, unless we are first persuaded of the fact of Jesus Christ. I think that we cannot claim that the Universe is made by such a God as the Christian theology presents, unless we are first sure that one of the things that has come into the world from that source is the life of Christ. There are some, I think, who would say that the historical fact is indifferent, the ideal remains valid; Christ is the revelation of God and of the true life for man, whether He existed as a historical fact or not. I cannot assent to that. If He never existed, where is the evidence that God is like Him? It is open to anyone to say that this character is supremely beautiful, but that unfortunately reality is constructed upon principles wholly at variance with it. But if that life is a fact, then, as we have said before, we have to conceive of God as One who can utter Himself in such language; we may go further and take it as the interpretation of the world, and then look again at the whole history of things; and we see (do we not?) that, in the ultimate analysis, the individual or the species has significance as it serves the progress of the race; and that moral development always means expansion of the area within which we owe service; and that political development, the growth of democracy, has always meant the growing insistence that each shall serve all. The spirit of absolute service may be seen in every field to be the actual spirit of the whole of life. But we should never have found that it was so, if it had not broken out once in its full splendour in the Person of the Lord, for only there is it seen in untainted completeness and beauty.

I said in the first lecture that in my belief the demand of reason that the world should appear coherent would stand over against the facts of experience in hopeless antagonism unless we accept the whole essential fabric of Christian Theology. And this is what I chiefly meant; the demand that the world shall appear rational led us to believe that it was all rooted in an Almighty Will; we cannot believe in an Almighty Will which, being entirely able to determine itself, does not will the good; we cannot believe that the world, which it has made, is good, unless the life of Christ was actually lived, and unless, with the sacrifice in which it culminated, it was indeed the revelation of the Father, and has in consequence a power to change our hearts and wills, making sin itself the means to the manifestation of the redemptive love, which is the true glory of God.

LECTURE VI

THE SPIRIT, THE CHURCH AND THE LIFE
ETERNAL

OUR Atonement is accomplished, and the
problem of evil solved, through the revelation
of the love of God in Christ. But how is it
possible for us in the twentieth century to
come under the influence of one who lived
two thousand years ago? How is it possible
that a life occurring at one moment of time
should have the immense influence that is
claimed for it upon the whole of human
history? If Christ is simply one isolated individual like any other individual, it is not
possible; apart from the doctrines of the Incarnation and of the Spirit, the whole experience
of Christendom is absolutely unintelligible.

There is no mockery more bitter than to
urge a man simply to follow the example of

Christ, if that is all that he is told. It is nothing to me that at about the same period Julius Cæsar conquered and regulated Gaul so masterfully in ten years that it remained permanently loyal to the Roman Empire. He could; I can't. It is nothing to me that St. Paul was caught away into the third Heaven and heard the unspeakable words, and spoke with tongues. He could; I can't. And if the example is all, it is nothing to me that Christ lived and died as no other man has lived and died. The very uniqueness makes the example all the more meaningless. He could; I can't. But if it is true that He is the Incarnation of the divine Word, of the principle by which God rules the whole of existence and through which He made the world, then it is made quite clear that I can never for an instant be outside His influence. It is the governing fact of all facts, and never for a moment can we be away from the divine purpose which is manifest in Christ. But then we may ask,—If it is true that the principle which is seen clearly in the life of Christ, and nowhere else so clearly, is after all the governing power in the whole world, what

is the need of the Incarnation ? It is governing the world already ; why should it appear
once for all in a human life ? Because the
work that is to be done is a spiritual work and
must, therefore, be accomplished through the
free assent of the people in whom that work
is wrought. So long as the power of God is
unnoticed, so long even as it is inadequately
understood, our response cannot be complete.
The divine power itself can only have the
effect upon human spirits which we call
redemption, if it wins from them freely a real
appreciation and assent; and, therefore, it is
necessary that something more than a mere
guiding principle should be given to us. What
we need is manifestation of the divine power
and the divine purpose such as will win from
our hearts free allegiance and answering love.
We need something upon which our imaginations can lay hold, something which will mould
our affections, something which will change our
will; and that can never be done except by
something that we can appreciate ; and we
cannot appreciate what is not before us. God
cannot be omnipotent except by the revelation
of His Love. By His power He could control

our actions, but not our wills. If He is to be
Lord of all that exists, He must be Lord of
our wills. But the will is not amenable to
force ; it can only be governed through what
seems to it good ; God can only rule our wills
through a complete and intelligible manifesta-
of His Love. The secret and hidden and
undetected operation of the Power of God
can never reach its own goal. If that goal is
to be reached, the divine Principle itself must
appear before us in all the splendour of its glory.
God can only be Almighty through the revelation of His Love—that is, through sacrifice ;
Calvary is the mode of God's omnipotence.

And so we reach a clue to the great paradox
which we found in all religious experience.
We found that in all religious experience we
are at once vividly conscious of our own
responsibility before God, and also of the fact
that all our lives are in His hands ; that He
guides and shapes our destiny from beginning to end ; that He is omnipotent yet we
are free ; and that remains an unintelligible
paradox, until we remember that the change
in man's will that is accomplished when love
is won from his heart by the love of another

is at once his own act and the act of the
other.   When St. Paul said, " I live, yet not
I but Christ liveth in me,"[1] he did not mean
that his will was suppressed and checked ; he
did not mean that either without his will, or
against his will, he preached the Gospel under
some strange compulsion ; he meant that his
life was wholly governed by Christ, because,
seeing the nature of Christ and the beauty
of His character, he had accepted that character freely as his own.   He was absolutely
governed by Christ; but it did not follow that
he was not free ; rather it followed that for
the first time he was perfectly free, for he had
freely yielded himself to the love of God and
in that yielding of himself had for the first
time found his own satisfaction and peace.

So it is in all our experience of God; we
are not driven on by some external force as
a mechanical body is set in motion by an
external force ; but love is won from our
hearts by the love of God.   We cannot resist
giving it, when we see the love of God ; but
what makes it impossible for us to resist is
just our human nature ; nothing else.   We are

---

[1] Galatians ii. 20.

free precisely in our inability to refuse our love.
It is the expression of our own nature ; it is
not something imposed upon us from without ;
it is the natural expression of what we are.

And so with the greatest difficulty, as it
sometimes seems, in the commencement of the
religious life ; people find that they cannot
approach God without His help, and then
they wish to pray for His help and find that
they cannot even pray without that help.
From the beginning to the end our lives are
in His hands absolutely.   But we are in His
hand as the child is guided by the love of the
Father, not as a physical object is moved by
an external force.   And the motion of our
wills which is wholly due to Him is none the
less the free motion of our own will : it is the
answer of our hearts to His love.   The true
conclusion to draw from the discovery of our
impotence is not a fatalistic quietism and
spiritual indolence, but a complete selflessness
and surrender to God.   This religious sense of
the individual's helplessness has not in history
led to inactivity, but to an energy that the
isolated individual could not command.

Now in this conception of a governing

divine Spirit which is in all the world, treated and interpreted as it is in the Christian theology, I believe we have the clue to the chief of our modern difficulties; for these difficulties, if I understand the matter aright, do not arise from any new way of thinking of specifically religious things. It is a change, not in our theology, but in our total habit of mind, to which we have to adapt ourselves; and this change is due to two main causes. The first is, of course, the development of natural science. A hundred and fifty years ago people supposed that God had made the world and had imposed certain laws upon it, and then left it to go more or less its own way according to those laws, interfering now and then by way of a miracle; and still we have in popular language certain events, usually, I am afraid, calamities, which are classified as the Act of God—a relic of that old way of thinking. Then gradually the development of science produced its effect upon the public mind, and men began to believe that everything can be explained by natural law. And very often religious people are distressed at this, for it seems to have curtailed the sphere of the divine activity. But it was they who had curtailed it in the first instance by allowing that it was only in miracle that we could see the hand of God. What has really happened to us is that instead of seeing the divine activity here and there, or now and then, we have again an opportunity of seeing · it, as we should always have seen it, everywhere and always. There is nothing which God does not do. "Through Him all things were made and apart from Him hath not one thing happened."

The growth of science, then, is one main factor in the situation; the other is the growth of democracy. As long as nations were governed by kings, it seemed natural to extend the analogy to the universe; men thought of God as King of the Universe; and I believe you will find that in all ages popular theology rests upon such political analogy. Then in the eighteenth century, when it was thought to be necessary to respectability that man should believe in the constitutional necessity of a monarch, but contrary to political prudence that he should be allowed to do anything, you have in theology the extraordinary phenomenon of Deism, which insisted strongly that God exists, but regarded it as fanaticism to suppose that He ever does anything. And now, in our time, we have a conception of Government as a power not acting upon the subjects from without, but through them from within ; a conception which maintains that the only power before which the individual should bend his will is the collective will of the whole community ; and parallel with that you have a great insistence on the doctrine, always in the Church from the outset, of divine immanence ; and when any preacher finds a way of expressing the divine immanence so that people can understand it, they crowd to him as to a new revelation. We must, I think, in our day, begin with this conception of the indwelling divine power, because it is at this point that we, like St. John, can find a starting-point common to ourselves and those to whom we speak ; but we must not end with it ; and we must not be content to leave it uncharacterised. We must not end with it, because as we said before, what is immanent in the world is the divine purpose, not the divine Will : an

immanent Will is nonsense. And we must
not leave it uncharacterised ; we must ask how
it operates, and to what goal it is leading us.
The answer for the Christian is the life and
death of Christ. " The Word was made flesh
and we beheld His glory." There is all the
difference in the world between the divine
principle of progress as mediated by nature or
by tribal worship or by secular civilisation
and that same divine principle mediated
through its own perfect manifestation in
Jesus Christ. When we have seen it manifest in Christ we can take it as the clue to all
our experience and see that in every depart-
ment of life the Spirit which was in Him is
operative. But if we had begun with biology
and human history we should never have
reached any conception of the governing
divine principle as one whose only characteristic is love, whose glory is moral, not
spectacular, and whose pre-eminence is
through sacrifice and not through power.
It is only through Christ that we can come
to the Spirit as the whole power of God
operating in its fulness upon our spirits. It is
indeed in all the world. The Word is the agent

of Creation ; it is in all the world, and we can never be altogether outside its influence ; but it will not have its full effect on our wills until we understand and appreciate it and yield ourselves to it ; that is to say until it has been fully manifest in the terms of our own life. So the Spirit proceeds, not only from the Father, but from the Father and the Son. We may look back upon the previous history of the world before Christ and see how the same Spirit, which was in Him, was guiding the ages up to Him, as it has guided the Church ever since. But in the fulness of its power it does not exist in the world till after the Incarnation and Crucifixion. "There was not yet Spirit, because Jesus was not glorified." [1]

The Spirit, therefore, which governs the world, must be mediated for us through Christ ; we must never for a moment suppose that we can find that same spirit anywhere else without His help. When we have found it in Him we may see its operation elsewhere. We cannot first find it elsewhere, and then discover that it was manifest in Him. For in

[1] John vii. 39.

all the rest of our experience there is no evidence that the character of the Spirit is the character of Christ; but if Christ is a fact, then, as we have often said before, the governing Power of the world must be something capable of expressing itself in that fact; it must be adequate to its own greatest achievement.

And so the Spirit is to be taken, not only as the guiding power of the world, but as the guiding power of the world as seen in Christ. Only so can it have its full effect upon our hearts and wills. No doubt the Spirit is present in all men—it " lighteth every man "; and it is no doubt more fully present in some who are not Christians than in some who are. But its full manifestation is in Christ alone ; others have the Divine Spirit in their degree, but He alone is altogether God. And though this or that man may reach great moral heights without any conscious relation to Christ, only the Love made manifest in the Cross is sufficient to take away the sin of the world.

And yet another condition is necessary ; the Spirit must be mediated through Christ, and it must be operative in the Church. The whole reason why this sort of discussion is necessary is that our religious experience always appeals for logical support; it is always anxious to defend itself against the charge of self-hypnotism; it wishes to know that the God revealed to it is not the object of a dream, but is the real and living God; that is to say, our religious experience knows itself to be precarious as evidence, and it appeals to philosophy for support; and a philosophical argument always fails to carry complete conviction to anyone who is alone in believing in it. I may think out some long train of reasoning which seems to me perfectly cogent; but if when I tell others they reject it, though I cannot see the flaw, I cannot help wondering whether there is not some flaw which they detect, though it escapes my notice. And so even when we have cor- roborated the evidence of our religious ex- perience by philosophical reasoning, we are still in a precarious position; we still need further support because we cannot be perfectly sure that our own reasoning is without flaw. We need, therefore, if our faith is to be absolutely secure that all men, nothing less, should come to believe what we believe. As long as there is one man who, after thinking the problem over, still doubts, there will be a haunting doubt in our own faith ; and, as a partial realisation of that universal support by all humanity, we collect together in the Church to support our own faith, because there we find other people who, either through the same reasoning, or from different reasoning, or else simply on the basis of their own religious experience, have reached the same conclusions as ourselves; and it strengthens our own belief in those conclusions to meet with others who have reached them. If the conclusions are untrue, the charge of mutual hypnotism can be made ; but if the conclusions are true, nothing in the world can be more rational than that we should take every possible step to secure that our belief in them is vital.

But there is more than this involved, for our belief does not end in intellectual assent; it must become a living faith, the impulse to a life singularly alien from our natural impulses. If this further step is to be taken, we need again the support of others—the support this time not so much of their intellects as of their wills, and above all of their affection. We need to consort with people all pledged to the realisation of the same ideal that we may catch their fire.

And then further we know quite well that any really living society is a far greater thing than the sum of the persons who compose it. England is not the name for the fact that a large number of us happen to inhabit a particular island; it is a spiritual entity with a life of its own, a life to which we all contribute in co-operation, but a life, none the less, greater than the mere sum of our own lives. Still more is it true that in the Church we have a great society professing an ideal which scarcely any, if any, of its members has ever realised, professing an ideal which probably not one of its members has ever fully grasped. Only in the whole Church is the whole truth known; only indeed when the whole Church is the same as the whole world will the whole truth be fully known; for each has his own contribution to make to the life which is to be lived under the impulse of the divine love; each individual

M

is unique and different from all others ; and as long as there is any who is withholding what he alone can give, that life remains imperfect.

But if all this is true, then it follows that in order to bring ourselves under the full operation of the Spirit we must be members of the Church, which is the Body of Christ, the organ of His Spirit as His fleshly Body was in the days of His earthly Ministry. It would take us far away from the fundamental questions that are occupying us in these lectures, if I were to go into details as to the exact meaning of the word "Church"; but at least it must mean this, a body with an intelligible form and definite organisation, to which we can consciously belong. It must not be a mere group of persons who happen to be congenial to one another ; that would be the narrowest conceivable sort of sect. It must be a full life, collecting together all the types of spiritual experience which can flow from the love of God ; and in our full membership in such a body, in devoting ourselves absolutely to its service, we shall be bringing our contribution to the whole life of the Body of Christ. That

Body of Christ is something which is steadily being built up. You will remember how, particularly in the later Epistles, St. Paul perpetually speaks about the building up of the Body of Christ, and the goal of it all is that we shall " come to one perfect Man," which will be the " measure of the stature of the fulness (or the completion) of Christ."[1] He does not mean, of course, that each of us is to become perfect in that sense, that each of us is to attain to the measure of the stature of Christ. Of course not. He means that the whole human race is to become so knit together through the purpose of God that it will be a single whole, with one life expressed through all its members ; so closely knit together that it can be called " one perfect Man " : and that will be the " measure of the stature of the fulness of Christ "; that will be the manifestation of the full glory of the Spirit of Christ : for if we limit the work of Christ to what He accomplished when He was upon earth, then that life becomes an isolated event and the rest of the world becomes an insoluble enigma. But if we say

[1] Ephesians iv. 13.

M 2

in that life there was manifest a principle which becomes increasingly manifest in the life of the whole world until at last the whole human race will exhibit the same character, then we see how the glory of Christ is not yet completely revealed and will only be known altogether when the whole world is showing it forth. He is the Head of the Body, and from Him " the whole body fitly joined together and compacted by that which every joint supplieth, according to the effectual working in the measure of every part, maketh increase of the body unto the building of it in love."

And from this point of view, may I suggest that we get a new impulse to the work of foreign missions? For we see that even our own faith can never be complete, and our lives never be under the full influence of the Holy Spirit, until the whole world is Christian. Only then will the Holy Spirit be active in the plenitude of His power.

Our conception of the world so far is that of a perpetual moral and spiritual progress, victory at every stage and always new victory to be won; and the impulse to all that progress is the love of God, at first dimly apprehended but in Christ fully revealed, so that now it operates in all its strength. And it all seems to have one fatal flaw; for men die before the victory, which might justify the effort of their life, is come; they die before they see the triumph of the cause for which they are themselves sacrificed. And so there is some element in the world, namely these men's experience, which remains still not quite rational, still not explained by the one divine Purpose. We need the doctrine of immortality. It is not enough that from the Father and the Son the Holy Spirit should proceed, nor that so proceeding He should operate through the Holy Catholic Church. We need also the Communion of Saints and the Life everlasting.

Now it is, of course, possible to treat the doctrine of immortality at very great length; and any brief treatment of it is bound to be almost provoking. And yet I will content myself with producing the argument which belongs to the general point of view we have adopted, and which, to my own mind, is the most convincing of all that can be urged on

the subject. It is this : we are thinking of
the world as the expression of the purpose of
God, for we found that without a divine will
in which the world is rooted and grounded
the whole of our experience is unintelligible ;
and we believe necessarily that that Will,
being perfectly free and untrammelled by any
sort of circumstance, will choose what is good ;
and we have found that even the world of our
experience may after all be regarded as part
of such divine Purpose, if we are willing to
take the principle that is manifest in the life
and death of Christ as the governing principle
of its existence ; and we have found also that
in this world every individual brings some
contribution of his own. Very well ; it is a
short step to say that that contribution must
not be lost. If it is lost, then some element
in the world is taken away, and the universe
is impoverished, which would be intelligible
enough if we were treating it as merely a
brute fact, but which is unintelligible if it is
nothing at all except the embodiment of the
divine Purpose. When you bring together
the Purpose of God and the uniqueness of
each individual soul, the doctrine of immor-

tality follows as a necessary corollary ; for it is impossible that God should allow the universe to be impoverished, and it is certain that the destruction of a unique, and therefore irreplaceable, spirit could be nothing other than its impoverishment. The love of God is the impulse of creation ; and that same love cannot allow the destruction of what it made for its own satisfaction. The love of God is the basis of our hope of immortality.

But if it is true that death is not the end of our life, but a change whose significance we cannot wholly estimate but which certainly does not exclude the individual from the spiritual society, then immediately it becomes true that we can pay the debts which we owe to the departed, because we can assist the progress of the Kingdom which includes both ourselves and them ; we can minister even to those, whom we perhaps have led wrong at some time or another and have never since met with that we might confess our guilt and help their recovery, because we can assist the progress of the Kingdom which includes both ourselves and them.

Thus the vision we win is of a spiritual

ity follows as a necessar corollary; for it
impossible that God hould the
verse to be impoverisht, and
t the destruction of a nique, a
e irreplaceable, spirit uld
er than its impoverishment. Th
d is the impulse of creatn; and
e cannot allow the deruction of
de for its own satisfaction. The
d is the basis of our hop of immoral
But if it is true that deat is not the
life, but a change whse significance
not wholly estimate but which
s not exclude the incividual from
ritual society, then immtiately it becom
e that we can pay the dots which we
the departed, because o can asst th
gress of the Kingdom wich includes
selves and them; we in minister
those, whom we perhaps ave led wrong
ne time or another and have never
t with that we might confess our guilt an
p their recovery, becate we can
e progress of the Kingdm which include
h ourselves and them.
Thus the vision we win of a

world, where perpetually new beings come into existence and none ever perishes, so that the volume of love, which is the pervading principle of this spiritual world, may grow and grow for ever; and what we witness is the perpetually wider application of the divine Word which God spoke in the cadences of Christ's life and death,—Cross and Resurrection, death and victory, life laid down and love triumphant.

That is the conception of the world which Christianity gives us, and the attitude of the Christian who has grasped this conception to the defiance, as it sometimes seems, of Reason, will be calm and collected; for some at least of the utterances which Reason hurls at Religion in a kind of desperate blasphemy, the Christian will accept as the very platitudes of the faith. When Reason says, "It is God who made all the world; He therefore is responsible; it is He who should suffer"; we answer, "Yes, of course; He does suffer; look at the Cross." And when Reason cries, "If God were the loving Father of whom you speak, He could not endure the misery of His children; His heart would break"; we answer,

"Yes, of course; it does break; look at the Cross." And when Reason exclaims, "God is infinite and ineffable; it is blasphemy to say we know Him; we cannot know Him"; we answer, "No; not perfectly; but enough to love Him; look at the Cross."[1]

And then we go on to compare this divine life revealed by Christ with our own conception of the ideal life for ourselves, and we find that it answers to our own ideal, differing from it only by transcendence; for when we put the question seriously to ourselves whether we would rather have a life of untroubled comfort and ease, or a life of struggle, even with suffering, against the evil of the world, there is no doubt what we would choose.

> What better would'st thou have when all is done?
> If any now were bidden rise and come
> To either, could he pause to choose between
> The rose-warm kisses of a waiting bride
> In a shut silken chamber, and the thrill
> Of the bared limbs bound fast for martyrdom?

If the martyrdom were no purposeless barren pain, but martyrdom for a great cause, martyr-

---

[1] This paragraph is taken substantially and almost verbally from *Christus Futurus* (Anonymous : Macmillan).

dom which is to do some good in the world,
which should we choose? Perhaps we do not
know which we should choose; but we know
which we should wish to choose; and we find
that our own ideal, our own conception of the
best life to live is after all just a feeble,
shadowy outline of the life divine as it is
revealed in Christ. The hypothesis, then,
meets the facts. Is there any other conception anywhere to be found which unites
the demand of Reason for a coherent and
intelligible universe with appreciation of all
the facts in life and particularly of evil and
suffering?

The Christian hypothesis meets the facts;
and it is not a hypothesis invented merely out
of men's heads in order to meet the facts. It
is an application to the world of a principle
that is already in the world, for it was in the
life of Christ.

We are trying in these lectures to think
scientifically about the world. I said at the
outset that the demand of Reason stands in
hopeless and irreconcilable antagonism over
against the facts of experience unless we will
accept the whole doctrine of Christianity—

unless, that is, we will accept the doctrine
that the world proceeds from God the Father,
the Creator; that the method by which He
creates and guides it is revealed in Christ and
particularly in His Death; the doctrine that
through that Life and Death the divine
power, in the Person of the Holy Spirit,
operates with full force through the Church
upon the individual, so constituting the
Communion of Saints, through entrance into
which we obtain Forgiveness of Sins, which
is the condition of the Resurrection and of
the Life everlasting. The whole creed is
the only hypothesis that meets the facts; no
article of it—not even the first—can stand
without the rest. No Spirit, no Christ; no
Christ, no God. Only the whole creed is
true; but that is true. As a hypothesis it
meets the facts, and it is no fictitious hypothesis, for its doctrines are all the register of
men's direct experience of God. Religious
experience and philosophy come into harmony and mutual support in the Christian
doctrine.

And then, as we look out upon the world,
we find it all knit together in the love of God.

From that love it all proceeds. It was because of that love that He made other spirits than Himself "to love and be loved by for ever." The world of spirits is perpetually growing and the volume of love grows with it. Love is made perfect through suffering in the struggle against the evil, which it permits in order that the glory of redemption may be known ; and we find in all our experience nothing but God, and the glory of God which is redemptive sacrifice.

HOLY, HOLY, HOLY, LORD GOD OF HOSTS ;
HEAVEN AND EARTH ARE FULL OF THY GLORY,
GLORY BE TO THEE, O LORD MOST HIGH.

THE END

THIS BOOK IS DUE ON THE LAST DATE
STAMPED BELOW

AN INITIAL FINE OF 25 CENTS
WILL BE ASSESSED FOR FAILURE TO RETURN
THIS BOOK ON THE DATE DUE. THE PENALTY
WILL INCREASE TO 50 CENTS ON THE FOURTH.
DAY AND TO $1.00 ON THE SEVENTH DAY
OVERDUE.

Lightning Source UK Ltd.
Milton Keynes UK
UKHW021631090119
335047UK00005B/206/P